CLIPPER
SHIP
MEN

BOOKS BY
ALEXANDER LAING

THE SEA WITCH
END OF ROAMING
WAY FOR AMERICA
FOOL'S ERRAND
WINE AND PHYSIC
SAILING IN
DR. SCARLETT
THE METHODS OF DR. SCARLETT
THE MOTIVES OF NICHOLAS HOLTZ
(WITH THOMAS PAINTER)
THE CADAVER OF GIDEON WYCK
(WITH THOMAS PAINTER)
HANOVER POEMS
(WITH RICHMOND LATTIMORE)

EDITED BY A. L.
THE HAUNTED OMNIBUS
THE LIFE AND ADVEN-
TURES OF JOHN NICOL,
MARINER

NEW YORK

CLIPPER
SHIP
MEN

By Alexander Laing

Illustrated by ARMSTRONG SPERRY

DUELL, SLOAN and PEARCE

COPYRIGHT, 1944, BY
ALEXANDER LAING

first edition

PRINTED IN THE UNITED STATES OF AMERICA

TO

AVIATION CADET PHILIP E. BOOTH
U.S.A.A.F.

CLIPPER SHIP MEN

CLIPPER SHIPS AND

CHAPTER ONE

A HUNDRED YEARS AGO THE PEOPLE OF THE UNITED States began peacefully to invade the whole world with an idea and an example. It was an astonishing performance. The virtues of political freedom had been growing throughout the first half-century of the young republic. Brimful and running over at the eastern seaboard, the American belief in personal liberty flowed outward until it mingled with the waters of every harbor on earth. Men were not perfect then: they are not ever. Much of America's bad went voyaging with the good. Yet it was the first time on human record that a powerful people had driven to the ends of the seas in great numbers and in peace.

There had been other outwellings of a particular national spirit, far over the waters. Navies of Rome carried the Roman idea and example to all shorelines that seemed worth the seizing for Caesar. Soon afterward, unknown to the land-hugging Romans, a heroic people from India spread their own idea of the good life over an area many times as great as the largest expanse of Caesar's little empire.

They were the Polynesians. With a skill unapproached for a thousand years by any other seafarers they captured the enormous Pacific.

Then the Arabs, driven by their Islamic faith, thrust westward into Spain, eastward to upper China and the Philippines. Of all the great early conquests, theirs was the most nearly peaceful. Their terrible fighting qualities became famous only when others tried to dislodge them with the sword from territories in which they had established themselves, more often than not, by virtue of the wisdom of their teachers and scientists, and the honest dealings of their business men.

The Portuguese took title to one half of the world, the Spaniards to the other half. They, and the late seafaring carriers of the idea of great empire—English, Dutch, French—battled almost to exhaustion. They fought somewhat with the aborigines, far more with one another, until they reached the great pause and comparative peace that came with Napoleon's downfall.

Today we have bitter reasons for supposing that a temptation to conquer the world by violence may never be extinguished. It seems all the more remarkable that the world conquest of our own great American dream could even have begun peacefully. This difference was not entirely due to the fact that our officials of government had little to do with it. The government of England had had little to do with the private companies of adventurers who had raised private armies and navies for conquest in the Sixteen Hundreds. Something had happened to the commercial community too, in free America. Our citizens, a hundred years ago, developed the first merchant marine competent to sail unarmed and unescorted, everywhere.

How did it happen, and why did it happen? What has become of that swift impulse to bind the world together mainly by the mutual benefits of trade? In earlier days, powerful nations had relied almost entirely upon plunder and slave-making, however politely disguised. In our own times, while too many among us were trying hard to look the other way, powerful nations returned to the disastrous folly of such methods. There was a while between, beginning in the Eighteen Forties, when the chance for a saner kind of world relationship was almost demonstrated by a peaceful people. Americans might have followed the usual pattern, designing new and more powerful men-of-war in which to go plundering. They built instead the first miraculous clipper ships. Most clippers carried nothing more bulky, in the way of armament, than what the skipper could lock up in a chest in his own cabin.

Today we again hold in our hands the bright stuff of a new era for mankind. Young Americans again are thronging to the world's farthest coasts. They are carried still, as they were a hundred years ago, by the swiftest mechanisms in existence. But this time they are not lightly armed.

Clippers of a new kind, the sky ships of our commercial airways, had been developed to the point where a new peaceful conquest seemed to be in the making, on the hundredth anniversary of our earlier one. But the sky-ship builders, the air-trail blazers, ignored the threat of others who were preparing to turn their good work to the uses of evil. Our first great chance to spread democracy peacefully around the world had collapsed because of internal evils which we were late in putting to rights, in our own country. Our spirit of freedom went abroad in the Eighteen Forties while there still was slavery at home. Generations of well-meaning men had tried to find ways around that central issue in American life. At last they had to face it, in the Civil War. Now once more, after a hundred years of looking inland, any family may be waiting for a son or a father to come home from the uttermost islands.

The young people of today, taking up with quiet courage a dreadful task put upon them by the shirking of their elders, at least know this: there can be no peace for the slave-makers, and no peace with them, at home or abroad.

This time, our great dream for a better world need not be made futile, as it was in the middle of the last century, because each man thought he had a right to keep at his own virtuous affairs and leave the righting of deep evils to somebody else.

Poised for a new adventure embracing the whole world, we would do well to look back at the records of that earlier one when the most ingenious of American devices were carrying our restless young men to England and Africa, China, India, and Australia. From those days we can learn something still about what lies deepest in the American spirit—about what is best, and also about what is dangerous, in our American nature.

The clipper-ship era made it plain that a young nation had suddenly come of age in seaboard America. The Yankee clippers took mankind by surprise, putting a value upon speed and ingenuity that had never been felt before. They were the first great evidence of the American method of turning the arts and sciences to practical work.

Something else in our national character cropped up in the clipper-ship era, to baffle the single-track historians who say that everything man makes can be accounted for by the number of dollars he thinks his gadget will earn. No-one who has read deeply into the records of the clipper ships, and of the men who made them, owned them, sailed them, can continue honestly to believe only that humdrum notion. It explains much. It does not explain all.

A historian with a more human touch, Lewis Mumford, has called the Eighteen Forties in America "The Golden Day." A lucky people, comparatively the luckiest and happiest on earth, felt that they had proved the rightness of the great dreamers and doers who had created a new nation. They had made mistakes. Too many of them were still trying to find ways of doing nothing drastic about the one intolerable mistake: slavery. But in the summing up they felt that they had done better than any other united people ever had done, getting a decent measure of dignity and happiness for the great majority of citizens.

American youth held up that example for the envy of the countries they visited. George Francis Train, an erratic but wholly American trader, wrote a number of books which reveal in their titles a typical crusading consciousness. *Young America Abroad*, which he published in 1857, and *Irish Independency*, issued eight years later, both are full of it. We find it often in the terse notes in log books, put down by young officers who did not share George Francis Train's self-confident flair for words, but who quite plainly shared his convictions.

What can we learn now from that first American effort to make an informal conversion of the world? How far did it succeed? Why did it fail in the end?

We are a people fond of tall stories and big ideas. But the time comes when we like to get down again to brass tacks. What about the brass tacks of the clipper-ship era, the cold figures?

Let us take some particular dates, and look at the records. Take 1825, the year in which the largest part of our foreign trade was carried in our own American ships: 92%. Take 1840, because it saw the beginning of the shipbuilding boom that soon was concentrating upon clippers. Take 1860 the year when the United States had a larger tonnage of merchant shipping than ever before, a maximum not reached again until recently. Take 1910, the year in which the smallest part of our foreign trade was carried in our own ships: less than 9%. What accounts for these ups and downs?

Between 1825 and 1840 our tonnage of ships in foreign trade rose slowly from two-thirds of a million to three-quarters. Then, in a swift upward rush for two decades the total increased to three times what it had been in 1840. Thereafter it sagged away until, in 1910, it was down about where it had started in 1840. During the last third of the Nineteenth Century, and the first decade of the Twentieth, years that seemed to be full of America's prosperous expansion, our interest in shipping fell until we had only the same tonnage in our merchant marine as we had had seventy years earlier, to participate in a commerce that had grown in the meanwhile almost fourteen times as great. These figures call for a better explanation than the common one that we were busy with the prairie schooner and the iron horse.

Look at it another way. Between 1860 and 1910 our population tripled, while our merchant marine dwindled to a third. An American boy thus had only about one-ninth the chance in 1910 that his grandfather had had in 1860 to engage in a career at sea, which more than any other could knit together the peoples of the earth.

Such a fact is one measure of America's lack of interest in world affairs, in the period just before the first World War. Perhaps it explains the unthinking zeal with which American youth turned again to the task, in 1917, of making the world "safe for democracy." Americans had forgotten what their ancestors had known—that it is necessary to be brave enough to live as well as to die for your beliefs. Our young soldiers, and far too many of their elders who should have been wiser, thought that the world could be made safe for democracy by the mere winning of a war.

This time there are few who believe in any such illusion. Nearly all of us know that the winning of the war will give us nothing more than a new chance to begin the task of spreading democracy. When the fighting is over we can take up again the peaceful side of the conquest, take it up where we left off in 1860.

All of the other sea-borne conquerors have wanted lands and plunder. After we call our warriors home we shall need to send some of them out again, in a new clipper-ship era of both the ocean and the air. It will be their task to conquer only the imagination of other peoples. If they can do that, we may be able this time to finish the task of making the world safe for democracy.

Democracy is a faith. If we are to conquer the world with our faith we can be helped greatly by the mechanical products of American genius. But the most beautiful of our new clippers of the air can do no more than to bring us to the ends of the earth. Our success when we get there will depend upon the ideas which we can succeed in leaving with other peoples. All that we are and were will otherwise pass like ships in the night sky. The world still will belong to those who can dream a stronger dream than ours, a dream more worthy of capturing the imagination of all men.

That is one reason why, in this book, the ideas that produced the clipper ships are more important than the ships themselves or their performances. It used to seem obvious, to all who fell in love with their memory, that the great American sailing ships of a hundred years ago had been the truest expression of the American spirit. Years from now, our present clippers of the air may seem to have surpassed them. Any such achievement ought to be judged against the other accomplishments of its own time. Yet there is a close link between the marine architecture of 1844 and the drafting boards of the designers of Pan American Clippers and Flying Fortresses. Problems of buoyancy and equilibrium, center of effort and streamlining, were being worked out then much as they are now. The designers of a hundred years ago have been given too little credit for their mathematics and physics. Slipshod writers have been pleased to spread the unworthy myth that the best sailing ships in the world were the lucky products of inspiration, or of trial-and-error.

Both factors contributed to the ultimate superb product. They still aid us. But the heart of the matter was then, and remains, an accurate knowledge of physical and mathematical laws. Old words of the wooden shipbuilders linger in the language of the airplane factories, describing parts of the job that are essentially the same. "Lofting," for example, is the job of enlarging the wing-sections drawn on a blueprint into accurate full-size patterns for the corresponding sections of the finished plane. Why is it called "lofting"? Because it is exactly the same job, in principle, as the one which was performed in the shipyard's mould loft, when the lines of the designer's model, section by section, were chalked large on the mould loft floor as guides for the making of full-size patterns of thin wood which the sawyers followed in cutting the timbers that would form the vessel's ribs. There is a picture of this process on page 183.

The materials change, but much of the method stays. Our flying clippers of the Nineteen Forties have their metal "plane" surfaces nearly parallel to the line of motion of the whole craft. The flying clippers of the Eighteen Forties had their canvas "plane" surfaces nearly perpendicular to the line of motion of the whole craft. The laws and reasons are the same for one as for the other. The problem in each case is to get, with a minimum of material and resistance, the maximum useful effort from a passing stream of energetic particles of air.

Sometimes we read the records of the great achievements of other days out of aimless curiosity. I think we do best when we read with the hope of discovering the things that are permanent in human nature. Nothing in these grim days has excited us to admiration more than the amazing true stories of a few men adrift for weeks upon the ocean when they have had to abandon their modern, ingenious ships of the air. Yet it is an old situation. The *Bounty* was a modern, ingenious ship in her own time, voyaging on a lofty, scientific endeavor. After the mutiny, her overcrowded launch was sailed 3600 miles to safety by her cast-off captain without the loss of a man.

The history of the things man builds is cold and stodgy unless it answers continually the running question: "Why?" And when we attempt to answer that question we are enriching our own present lives. We are dealing, not with mere dead facts, but with ideas that are still usefully alive.

All the great conquests have been driven by ideas. Those that have been driven by cruel and greedy ones have endured only so long as the conquerors could keep up the harsh fight to hold what they had taken.

Perhaps, after this lapse of a hundred years, we can take up again the peaceful conquest begun by our clipper-ship men in America's golden day. Let us go back, and learn more about ourselves by finding out what kind of men they were.

CHAPTER TWO

Even at great moments, our lives are likely to be made up of a succession of usual little happenings. The young bombardier, in his first run over an enemy objective, is obsessed with the clockwork details of piloting his fighting ship of the air, during the moments while he acts as her commander. And the pilot himself, responsible for all the rest of the death-haunted journey, is too busy with his dozens of little instruments to give much thought to the heroics of his task.

A hundred years from now, will it be possible to describe such a journey—a thousand miles through the rainy dark from base to objective and back—unless attention is given to the little human routines which alone make it possible?

The bare, incredible outlines are like those of Jason's voyage between the clashing rocks, or the Polynesian legend of Maui fishing up islands from the bottom of the sea. It is all clearly explainable, if we remember the radio beam, the altimeter, the bombsight. Without them it becomes fabulous at once.

Some of the achievements of the clipper ships have been regarded as fabulous by honest, experienced seafaring men who gained their own practical experience at a later date in other vessels. Who is to be trusted, the man who says he saw a thing happen, or the one who did not see it and says that it could not have happened? All history is made from the records left by eyewitnesses. The test of their truthfulness usually is made by checking up on the little details in the record.

Those are two reasons for getting down to brass tacks when we tell over again the stories of great achievements. The little details make the big results more understandable, and they are a check upon the general accuracy of the account.

Let us live over again the last couple of hours of one of the greatest days in the history of sail, in one of the greatest of sailing ships. In doing so, we shall have to keep an eye on the minor matters set down in her log book by her mate.

At ten o'clock on the morning of March 17th, 1853, the clipper ship *Sovereign of the Seas* was slashing her way among enormous combing waves of the South Pacific, headed for Cape Horn. All night she had roared along under her royals, defying such boisterous rain squalls as would have scared any skipper afloat, a few years earlier, into snugging down to reefed topsails, for fear a sudden gust would drive his ship like a sounding whale beneath the next wild mountain of water. But Captain Lauchlan McKay had a new kind of sailing machine under his heels—a ship that rode the waves more steadily, and remained drier, the faster she drove. He had no worries about her buoyancy. His wits were busy with the state of affairs aloft, amongst her sails and spars.

Something was happening which never had happened in the world before. McKay knew it. He hung on to his canvas heroically, watching the slack lee rigging that betrayed the extent to which the weather shrouds were stretched by the terrific strain. The *Sovereign of the Seas*, the largest sailing ship afloat, required masts more than a yard in thickness at the deck. These were made up of several pieces, bound together with thick iron hoops—but the grim power of the wind was wrenching them apart, "springing" them, as the seamen said. The fore topmast was cracked wide open in two places. The main topmast, when the ship heeled down, shrieked like a giant whose muscles were being torn from his bones.

Twice, and then twice more, the ship's bell struck. The mate and two seamen stepped down the slanting deck to the lee quarter. One of the foremasthands carried a long reel wound with quarter-inch hemp line. The other had something which looked like a small hour-glass. Actually it held just enough sand to run through in fourteen seconds. At the end of the hemp line there dangled a wooden chip cut to the shape of a generous helping of pie. The curved part of the pie-shaped chip was weighted with enough lead to make it float straight up and down in the water. The end of the line ran through a hole near the point where the middle of the pie would have been, and was knotted behind to hold it. From the other two corners, two pieces of cord dangled, connected together by a plug.

The mate fitted the plug into a socket lashed to the log line a couple of feet above the chip. When he suspended the device, the chip swung exactly at right angles with the line itself, held in that position by the pair of cords. Bracing his feet, the man with the reel steadied it before him at arm's length, shoulder high, gripping the two handles. It spun around as the mate pulled off a few loose loops of line, said, "Watch!" sharply, and heaved the chip overboard.

The seaman with the glass echoed, "Watch, sir," keeping it ready. The reel whirred as the chip sank vertically in the water and was swept astern. The officer, his arm moving as fast as it could go, helped the line along with quick pulls until a scrap of white rag, fastened into the strands of hemp, came from the reel. This indicated that the chip had passed far enough astern to lie beyond the disturbed water of the ship's wake. Just as the white cloth marker whipped over the tafferel, the mate shouted, "Turn!"

The seaman inverted his fourteen-second glass immediately and answered, "Done, sir."

The officer stood with his hand hovering over the line, rapidly counting, "*One—half—two—half—three—half—*" as more little markers of leather and cord flashed by.

When the sand ran out, the man with the glass called, "Stop!"

The mate clamped both his hands upon the line. Far astern, this sudden strain yanked out the plug which had held the chip vertical in the water. It leapt a little, then skittered on the surface. Hauling in some slack, the mate verified his count of the number of markers which had been taken off the reel. His grip had closed near one of the leather half-knot marks. The next even marker aft proved to be a piece of cord with nine knots tied in it. These knot-markers were located about 47½ feet apart. The amount of line which had followed the white rag over the rail thus was 9½ x 47½ feet. The *Sovereign of the Seas* had traveled 451¼ feet through the water to drag out that amount of line in the 14 seconds while the sands were running through the glass.

Working it out by proportion, you will see that she had been tearing along at a rate of 1934 feet a minute. Multiply by 60 minutes, and you get 116,040 feet an hour, or 22 miles, as landsmen measure miles. But sailors put 800 more feet in a mile than landsmen do, in order to make a sea mile equal to about one degree of longitude near the equator. Therefore the ship had been sailing, when the log was cast, at 19 nautical miles an hour.

That was part of the miracle. So far as the people on board her knew, nobody ever had sailed at that rate of speed before. Their ship was going so fast that they had had to use a special trick to be able to measure her speed. If they had been aboard an ordinary vessel, or if light breezes had been wafting the *Sovereign of the Seas* herself along, the time interval would have been measured with a standard 28-second glass. The line had been made for use with one of them, and the actual number of knots taken off the reel in 28 seconds would have shown the speed directly in miles per hour.

But the *Sovereign of the Seas* could reach a speed which no-one had ever dreamt of when log lines were perfected. All the line on the usual reel would have been pulled off before the sands of a 28-second glass could have run through. Consequently her builder, the skipper's brother, who had deliberately designed her to be the fastest ship afloat, had put a fourteen-second glass aboard her for use when she was reeling off more than fifteen knots.

In this case, at ten o'clock in the morning of March 17th, 1853, the mate did not have to go through the mathematical processes by which I have tried to explain how the log line worked. He merely multiplied the observed result of 9½ knots by two, to make up for the fact that the fourteen-second glass had cut the usual time interval in half.

"Nineteen knots again, sir," he reported to Captain McKay.

The skipper nodded grimly and said, "Now you may take the royals off her, mister."

The mate repeated the order with relief and walked to the break of the quarterdeck to station men at the halyards. The royals bellied as the yards came down on their lifts.

Then the sails bunched up like breakfast rolls when the clewlines hauled the lower corners of the sails up chock to the blocks at the centers of the yards. Three Polynesian boys went aloft and laid out on the weather yardarms to fist and skin the bulging canvas up on the yard, lashing it with gaskets passed up over the top from aft, and down on the forward sides.

When all was snug, the mate went below to the log slate in the chart room. The "slate" was really a small table, with white lines painted on a black top. Opposite the hour 10 in the left hand column he chalked the figure 19. A glance up the column verified the fact that it was the third hour at which the log had shown a rate of 19 knots. Looking higher he saw that for each of the five hours beginning at three in the morning she had made 18 knots. From 4:00 P.M. through 2:00 A.M. a steady rate of 17 had been maintained. Counting again, to check the memory of his last count, he knew that unless there was a catastrophe before noon the miracle was going to occur.

There was no catastrophe. The furling of the royals had relieved the strain aloft just enough. But the lunging seas piled higher and higher. Gray-green waves in the deep South Pacific, blurred always at the top where the wind rips the upper skin of water into vapor, are given a chance to roll all the way from New Zealand: thousands of miles with not even a reef to get in their way. The *Sovereign of the Seas* was driving about as fast as the waves themselves. The crest of an enormous comber occasionally would catch up with her just as it broke into acres of foam, and would slue her sidewise off her course. Then she would drop dizzily into a deep valley between the wet mountains thundering all around her. That would shut off part of the force of the wind.

Nevertheless, when six bells were struck and the log again was cast, her speed proved to have slackened by only one knot. The captain and mate looked at each other and knew that their miracle had occurred. For the first time in the world's history a ship had sailed more than 400 sea miles in 24 hours.

And there was an hour still to go before midday.

The *Sovereign of the Seas*, when her great captain drove

[19]

her to this great record, had been less than a year afloat. Vessels of her class, true clipper ships, had been developed only within the decade. At about the time when the keel of this one was being laid at East Boston, the editor of *Harper's Magazine* wrote in his comment on events of the day that he could not "of a surety pass by that new burst of exultation, which is just now fanning our clipper vessels, of all rig and build, into an ocean triumph."

Americans had a right to feel exultant. Their young nation's shipbuilders and designers had boldly junked most of the accumulated ideas of nations that had been building ships for a thousand years. In less than a decade they had proved their new ideas right by producing scores of ships that were better than any ever seen in the world before.

The achievements of the clippers themselves have been described superbly in at least two books of permanent value. Taken together, they can hardly be improved upon. One is called *The Clipper Ship Era*. It was published in 1910, and written by Captain Arthur H. Clark. The other, *Greyhounds of the Sea*, is the work of Carl C. Cutler, and was brought out in 1930.

Captain Clark had sailed in some of the famous clippers when he was a boy. He wrote from experience of the ships themselves. Mr Cutler had also had a deep-water apprenticeship in square sail of a later period, but he wrote more from knowledge gained by wide research. He dug into more of the records, corrected many of the errors that had been current, and added a vast number of verified new facts. Captain Clark gave us a vivid and authentic first-hand picture, accurate for the most part, but somewhat dependent upon memory. Mr Cutler expanded the picture, and put most of the discoverable facts and figures on record in excellent chronological lists. His book can be referred to for information about hundreds of particular ships—for news of their builders, their masters, their performances.

Those who want the story of *what* happened should read Clark and Cutler, in that order. Both books splendidly describe the great ocean races when the clippers dashed and bucked around watery tracks ten or twelve thousand miles almost neck and neck all the way. Cutler and Clark have left us little to write about except the great question: "Why?" Clark, the reminiscent good reporter, is not particularly interested in that question. Cutler gives many of the answers, but he limits himself to fairly recent times.

As I see it now, most of the clipper ship books have started too late to explain the miracle against a meaningful background, as if one could begin the story of aviation with the Wright brothers. They were the first who flew successfully, over and over again. But many others gave their lives to the project in earlier days.

This book tells the story of man's effort to imagine the perfect ship. It tries to tell why the dream was shaped in certain ways, in earlier ages, in order to show how it finally came to perfection in a few such ships as the *Sovereign of the Seas.*

CHAPTER THREE

THE SPIRIT OF A PEOPLE REVEALS ITSELF PLAINLY IN their handiwork: in Egyptian pyramids, Roman roads, Gothic cathedrals. We in the United States can point to our skyscrapers as something entirely our own, engineered and put together by Americans for American reasons. Although other countries have copied them, and have built a few, they were our idea to begin with. We have stuck hundreds of them upwards into the heavens, often in places where they were not really necessary. Egyptians piled up pyramids which were not really necessary either. Part of the spirit of Egyptian religion is expressed in the pyramids. Skyscrapers express our American spirit, our almost religious respect for a certain kind of achievement, solid and lofty. They advertise to the world the ingenuity of a people who refuse to admit that any mechanical problem is too large or too intricate. And the shape of them is the shape of the American dream.

Even so, when I look at the New York skyline from the bay, it always seems to me that these buildings are mere stone monuments we have set up in the memory of the greatest American achievement of all. If you compare the best examples of set-back architecture with the sail-plan of a clipper "flying all her kites" you will see that the building is almost a model of the ship. The word "skyscraper" would have surprised nobody on the New York waterfront a hundred years ago, because the building has borrowed its very name from that of a lofty sail. Skysails, when cut in a triangular shape, were called skyscrapers as long ago as 1794.

Of these two objects that look so much alike in outline, I think that the clipper is the better example—the perfect symbol—of the American dream. The clipper ship was perhaps more of a miracle in its day than the skyscraper is in ours. It came first, which is one reason for giving it first place. Ninety-odd years ago American clipper ships—new, swift, and leanly beautiful—sped out by the hundreds to represent American methods in every nook and back-alley of the trading world.

What was the need, in the first place, for such ships as the *Sovereign of the Seas?* Who brought them to perfection so quickly, once the need was felt? Why did they so quickly disappear?

Who invented the clipper ship?

No-one, of course. The glory of all great symbols,

whether pyramids, or cathedrals, or something else, lies in the fact that they are the perfect expression of the long hopes of many men—the shape of a whole people's dream.

"THE BUILDING IS ALMOST A MODEL OF THE SHIP"

No single man invented even a major part of the principle of cathedral architecture. The same fact is true of the principles of marine architecture that were brought to their miraculous climax in our clippers. Toward the end of the long process, a few men can be singled out who made definite, large contributions. One man—the builder of the

Sovereign of the Seas—gathered together the work of many others into an all but perfect balance at last. That man, Donald McKay, proved himself the greatest genius of wooden shipbuilding by producing more first-rate examples than anyone else has ever done.

Yet even Donald McKay was not an inventor of importance. He can be described with more fairness as having been something like the Henry J. Kaiser of his times: a genius in manufacturing, in simplifying, in adapting and balancing the skill of many workers and many contributors of ideas. Behind Donald McKay the history of the clipper extends back as far as you want to go. It is impossible to choose any date and say, "The last ship launched before that day was not a clipper, the next one was a clipper." Instead, over a period of two or three decades, ships changed slightly, taking on more and more of the characteristics which we now think of as being typical of the clippers and not typical of older vessels. Around 1848, the clipper ship was established as a type. Everyone knew then what "clipper ship" meant. A few years later the type had been brought to perfection. Before 1860 the last one of all had been launched.

If we really want to know where the idea of the clippers came from, how they were perfected, and why they vanished, we have to look back through the long history of the sea. Although the clippers were merchant ships exclusively, we cannot understand all of the forces which helped to produce them unless we explore too the history of fighting ships and naval tactics in battle.

Look in the sky today and the reason will be clear. Our aircraft, hurrying to a hundred fighting fronts, show many changes made to adapt them to new tasks and new conditions. In a peaceful tomorrow, some of these changes will be dropped. It will no longer be necessary to mar the streamlining and lower the speed, with transparent plastic blisters for the gunners. But other developments will be as useful in peace as in war. Many of them would not have been made so quickly in peace time.

Men do not dream of things until a need fills them with longing. What made men quite suddenly discontented with the centuries-old idea of a good ship, and set them to hoping for a better one? Tyrants had a great deal to do with it. Oppressed peoples saw that they could not hope to use sea power in winning their freedom unless the few ships which they themselves might make would be better and faster than the average ones belonging to tyrants who could afford to rely on the mass power of fleets and the force of numbers.

The tyrant Hitler, with his standardized *Luftwaffe* of good enough planes in vast numbers, probably was stopped from a quick world conquest by nothing but the sheer excellence of Britain's much smaller Royal Air Force of Spitfires and Hurricanes. The history of tomorrow's triumphant aircraft will be traced back, not so much to the multitudinous Heinkels and Messerschmitts of tyranny, as to the heroic ingenuity that won the Battle of Britain in the sky.

For similar reasons we ought to seek the beginnings of the clipper ship at least as long ago as in the fierce efforts of Dutch and English shipbuilders to defeat the power of the great Spanish fleets in the Sixteenth Century. The final, mounting wave of improvement which produced the clippers really began to form in such another period, when Americans were freeing themselves from England, the greatest seapower of 1775.

Joshua Humphreys, who built *Old Ironsides*, died some years before the first of the famous clippers was launched. His frigates had little resemblance to the final clipper ships, but a new kind of thinking went into the Humphreys designs, and it is fair to say that the last continuous era of improvement, that resulted in the clippers of the late Eighteen Forties, was given its first great movement forward by Humphreys, fifty years earlier.

There is even a curious probability that the use of steam engines, on railroads rather than in ships, may have had a good deal to do with the designing of sailing ships that were much faster than any ocean-going steamers of their day.

Great ideas often flame up from a little spark of thinking, nursed along for centuries by queer fellows, seemingly to no good purpose. Presently the times are ripe to add fuel, and blow, and make the idea bright enough for the whole world to see. The steam engine probably began at about the time of Christ in the form of a little toy called the aeolipyle. The world thinks of James Watt as having invented it in the days of King George III, but Watt only added improvements that made the older kinds of engines really useful.

That was what happened too in the case of clipper ships. But before the world could expect the speed of merchant vessels to be increased, it first had to decide that speed itself was a virtue. That in itself is a recent idea. For a proper background we have to accustom ourselves to a notion bewildering to the modern American mind: the medieval idea that speed itself is of no importance.

In earlier days, men thought the oceans had an edge off which they might tumble. They believed that success to their ventures came from a friendly god's help, rather than from the good design in their vessels. Offshore waters were uncharted, dangers unmarked. Speed in consequence was a very doubtful virtue. The early, rough charts showed even most coastlines many miles out of their true positions, and did not bother to indicate reefs and shoals at all. With such guides to sail by, it is no wonder that seamen were content to frog along at a slow pace which would keep them from hitting too hard when they did run upon an obstacle, which was fairly often.

Back in those early days, we can catch the first gleams of ideas that had to wait for such practical aids as good charts before even an adventurous shipowner could see any sense in owning anything so obviously suicidal as a fast ship.

CHAPTER FOUR

SOME OF THE OLDEST HUMAN RECORDS FROM EGYPT, Assyria, and China tell us of efforts to catch the wind in sails. Shipbuilding is an ancient industry, and has always been among the largest. That being the case, only such factors as the lack of charts can explain why the world should have waited over five thousand years for a really intelligent effort to perfect the sailing ship.

In a modern world full of gadgets and things that run with motors, we sometimes forget that in earlier times men were just as clever as we are. Certainly they were at times wiser than we are, which is a different thing. Greece in the age of Pericles might have made the clipper ships. Greece had great scientists and craftsmen. She had tools and materials as good as those in use here a hundred years ago, when the clippers were born. But the Greeks had other interests, and believed in different gods. Their kind of life did not make them feel a need for fast ships. They preferred to express their quieter genius in immortal statues. Among our gadgets and motors, it is healthy for us to remember that nobody since the days of Pericles seems to have been able to equal that ancient Greek genius for statuary.

The rules of shipbuilding are a form of architecture. Most of the scientific principles of architecture on land were developed long before the birth of Christ. For sheer brilliance of engineering, the greatest modern structures are no more remarkable than the cathedrals of the Middle Ages. The one at Amiens, for example, standing 360 feet high, is a delicate structure of stone and glass that has remained staunch for seven centuries—proving that the master craftsmen of France did not need such modern trickery as steel girders to hold a vast and lofty edifice together. They studied the scientific principles of arches and buttresses, and made great curving roofs of stone with nothing to hold the stones together except good design and the pressure of the individual stones against one another.

The men who created those miraculous buildings could have fashioned the clippers, if they had wished, but they were moved to express their genius in other ways. Any great invention or development of human handiwork has to reflect the interests of most of the people in its time and place. This gives us another clue to the reason why the ultimate development in shipbuilding came so late. It was because merchants were the last class of people to realize the wisdom of hiring the best scientists and artists to work for them. It has been a late discovery in the history of strictly practical affairs that the gods and the money-changers are not responsible for everything—that there also are clear scientific and artistic truths behind every kind of human activity.

All down the ages until about a hundred years ago, the sailing ship seems to have been developed by plain, stupid trial-and-error. The human product most frequently shattered and built anew and shattered again, the one that consequently offered more chances than any other for working out fresh ideas, wallowed along with little important improvement from the days of the earliest Pharaohs to the times of Queen Elizabeth. There seems to have been nothing like the effort we find in other fields of endeavor—such as the building of cathedrals—to get at true artistic and scientific principles and to apply them with the least effort, the greatest effectiveness. Civilized men simply took it for granted, for centuries, that if the wind blew against them they could do nothing but anchor, or "lie to" and wait for it to shift astern. Yet the mathematical and mechanical problem of sailing against the wind was simple, compared with that of building a stone cathedral roof more than a hundred feet in the air without steel girders.

No record has been kept of the exact facts about some of the trends we should like to study. But words themselves often give us clues. Memory of the heroic days of sail has hung on so strongly to our hearts that today when we want to honor the latest miracles of aviation we can think of no words more suitable than "Skyliner" and "Yankee Clipper." How many of us remember as we use those terms that the first "liners" were New York sailing ships of the Black Ball Line, and that the real Yankee clippers were sailing ships too?

The way in which words have been used and changed often reveals the truth about things that would otherwise be lost to us. Take for example the words used to describe the method of finding the speed of the *Sovereign of the Seas* on her record-breaking run. The process was called "casting the log," yet the thing actually cast overboard was called a "chip." The phrase "casting the log" originated in days when it really described the process. One of the earliest ways of reckoning a ship's speed was to cast a log overboard from the bows and count the number of seconds that passed until it reached the stern. Knowing the ship's length, the sailors thought they could reckon her speed in miles per hour by seeing how long it took to sail the distance of her own length past a floating log. The trouble was that the ship disturbed the water so much that some of it was swirled in circles or dragged along with her. Therefore the log did not drop astern fast enough to show the true velocity. The log-line method was presently developed, to let the log float past into smoother water before beginning the measurement. It was hard work to pull a log back to the ship, so the chip was invented. But sailors long had called the process "casting the log." They refused to change it to "casting the chip."

Nowadays, most ships' "logs" are little gadgets like the speedometer on a car, spun around by a kind of propeller trailing at the end of a wire over the stern. They are called "patent logs" to distinguish them from the old type. We still use the word "log" in referring to a device that no longer has any relationship to a piece of wood.

Hundreds of seagoing words have drifted ashore into our everyday language. I have heard a man say, as a car sped by, "They must have been reeling off eighty miles an hour," but I am sure he had no idea of how a log line is "reeled off" on board a ship. The phrase "chock to the blocks," which I used in the second chapter as seamen use it, also has come ashore as "chockablock." Block is the nautical form of the landsman's pulley. Chockablock at sea means that something has been hoisted tight up against the block itself. On land we forget about the block part of it, and use it as often as not to mean something crammed full.

By tracing back the history of one word that behaved in an opposite manner—a landlubber word which went to sea and stayed there—we come to an important reason why men started to try to improve the speed of ships. This word, as we hear it now at sea, is pronounced "fo'c's'le," or "foak-sull" but it is still spelt "forecastle." Usually it means the space in which the sailors live, which always used to be the foremost part of the ship and in many cases still is. Late in the sailing-ship days the "foremasthands" sometimes were quartered in a deck house placed aft of the foremast. In modern tankers and grain ships, their living quarters frequently are in the extreme after part of the vessel. But the speech of sailors is hard to change: they still call the place where their bunks are the "fo'c's'le," even if they are right over the rudder, as was the case in the S.S. *Sucarseco* in which I once made a voyage.

One thing that can be said with assurance about sailors'

quarters for the last three or four centuries is that they had no resemblance whatever to the grandeur of a "castle," either in structure or in furnishings. In the days of the Spanish Armada the stern or poop was not unlike a castle in appearance, but the "fore" castle was even lower than it is today. As a rule it was the part of the ship closest to the water. How then did it get its name?

For an answer we have to go still farther back, to the Middle Ages, where we find references to both forecastles and aftercastles, with pictures in manuscripts and paintings to show that the words meant just what they said. The "fore" castle was a little fortress built at the forward end of the ship, and the "after" castle was another one of about the same size and shape built over the stern. They were used as were castles ashore: as high, safe places from which to pour unpleasant things on the head of your enemy. Naval warfare, before the development of cannon, was almost entirely a matter of boarding the enemy and capturing his fortresses.

Little islands along the coasts were equipped in the same way, with castles often rising sheer from the water's edge. Ships were castled floating islands which could be moved up alongside the enemy. If your castles were higher than his, you had the advantage. That is one reason why shipbuilders of the Middle Ages did not bother much about speed. In order to balance tall castles fore and aft, a ship had to be wide and steady. To get greater speed, for hunting the enemy down, the ship had to be made longer and narrower, with lower castles. But lower castles meant that the enemy had the advantage when you did catch up with him, and could drop his firepots and boiling oil on your

THE "GREAT MICHAEL," FIFTEENTH CENTURY

head. That, sensibly perhaps, was considered the most important point.

Even earlier than "fore castle" we find the term "fore stage." Wood-carvings in churches, old coins, and the official seals of seaside cities, show little ships with "stages" or platforms erected on poles at both ends: the beginnings of forecastles and aftercastles, but not yet fortified or made solid as they later were.

The idea of a warship as a steady little island with castles on it influenced the designers of merchant ships as well. Most of them were built to defend themselves against pirates or political enemies. The wider they were the more cargo they could carry. Anyway, nobody was in much of a hurry in those days.

It was gunpowder that changed the picture. The early ways of destroying a ship were to ram it or burn it. Greek fire, a chemical forerunner of gunpowder, was sometimes spouted from gunlike tubes in the sea fights of the Middle Ages. The later development of guns which could send heavy shot for several hundred feet made the old "fore" and "after" castles more of a target than a protection. Gradually they were cut down until the fore castle disappeared altogether as an object and survived only as the name of the forward part of the deck. Seamen took the word over and gave it to the space below the foredeck, although it had formerly meant a structure built above the deck.

When cannon came into general use on war vessels, the amount of sail began to be increased. More of it was used fore and aft of the mainmast. Ships were built longer and lower. These changes gave them more speed but made them slower in turning. Consequently the leverage of the sails was increased by means of a long bowsprit and an extra mast or two aft. These partly made up for the greater difficulty of turning a narrower ship as compared with the

THE "HENRI GRACE À DIEU," LAUNCHED 1514

old ones that were almost bowl-shaped under water. They also added to the vessel's speed and steadiness.

Formerly, a naval battle had begun when opposing ships grappled and one was able to send its men to board the other. Soon that feature became the last move in the conflict, after the guns had battered one or the other enemy into helplessness. Under these new conditions, it became

[37]

more important to use the wind efficiently, both to get into position to deliver a well-directed broadside, and, from the other point of view, to be able to dodge or get out of range.

Thus this particular change in the habits of naval warfare, wrought by gunnery, had to come about before the usefulness of speed and quick maneuvering in a fight could be fully appreciated.

There were other considerations. In the south of Europe slaves were cheap, and rowing seemed a more reliable means of propulsion than sailing. Sweeps, as the longer oars were called, were still in use in small naval vessels as late as our own war of 1812. Throughout most of the six-thousand-year history of sailing ships, indeed, the average vessel was designed principally for rowing. Sails were added to help out when the wind happened to be favorable and not too strong or too light.

There is an absolute limit to the speed at which human beings can row a large vessel. It cannot be made to go faster than the oar blades can be moved by human strength. The light racing shells used in the college regattas today, with no room for cargo—craft that are useless in any but the smoothest weather—can sustain a maximum speed of only 12 knots. The best sea-going galleys of the Middle Ages are said to have been rowed half as fast as that in a brief emergency. With sails looked upon only as something to help the rowers along, and not to be relied upon except in cases of luck, there was no point in trying to design vessels that could sail faster than they could be rowed.

So it happened that men living in the same times which saw the building of the great cathedrals took little or no interest in developing marine architecture to a similar excellence. What improvement there was in the sailing qualities of ships, up until about a hundred years ago, was provided as often as not by smugglers and pirates. The truly great brains were employed at other kinds of work. Mankind did not have much respect as yet for machinery—and it should not be forgotten that a sailing ship is a machine.

Now, as we near the middle of the Twentieth Century, every boy seems to be in love with the shining machines that enter so much into all our living and dying. In the driver's or pilot's seat, or even when nursing a few extra revolutions from the sputtery outboard motor on a homemade sea sled, the boy feels himself connected to the machinery, as if the nerves from his brain passed out through the ends of his fingers and into the controlling mechanisms. His mind sees and knows what is happening through solid metal or plastic when the plug fails to fire or the commutator sparks too much.

Except that the machines were different, boys of a hundred years ago were much the same. The feeling of being part of the machine is older than airplanes or automobiles or outboard motors. No-one ever knew it better than the royal boy, lying out on the weather yardarm to fist a sail, or the skipper whose brains were also the brains of a living creature of wood and canvas that skimmed along between wind and water. That feeling of blending into the machine was what made sailing ships possible, and still does. But in the early days, men seem to have regarded ships as animals operated by the gods. Only slowly, and much later, did men come to think of themselves as part of the machine called a ship.

CHAPTER FIVE

THE DREAM COMES FIRST. WHEN ENOUGH PEOPLE FIND themselves dwelling upon a great idea, presently some men will fall in love with the dream and give their lives to the job of making it come true. The triumphant and terrible dream of our own days—human flight—is as old as history. The story of Daedalus of Crete, who made wings for himself and his son Icarus, has inspired many men.

Leonardo da Vinci longed for wings, and published plans of flying machines in the year 1505. Many others, over the next few centuries, risked their necks in winged contraptions for the sake of that ancient hope. With better luck and materials, some of their contraptions would probably have worked. Motorless gliders nowadays can be kept in the air for hours at a time. In 1842, when the clipper-ship era was dawning, an Englishman named W. S. Henson patented an engine-driven flying machine, but the world had to wait for lighter engines before such a machine as Henson's could have a chance of carrying men aloft at their will. An American named Langley had built a practical flying machine before the Wright brothers built theirs, and a Frenchman named Ader had flown a little way in a similar machine. But we still say that the Wright brothers "invented" the airplane because they found out how to make one that would reliably do what was expected of it.

The same sort of slow progress led up to the sudden rush of activity which produced America's canvas-clouded fleet of clipper ships. Looking backward, men later tried to decide which was the first clipper. It was as hard as it is to tell at exactly what point a gradually widening river becomes a bay.

Yet it probably was the invention of engines, as much as any other cause, that finally gave the world its perfect sailing ships.

By "engine" I do not mean only the kind that turns wheels or propeller shafts. In the days of the first practical steamships, "engine" took on a new meaning: the one we most frequently think of when we use the word now. But it was only then, about a century and a half ago, that it began to mean a kind of machine which could run by using energy produced inside itself. In medieval times, anything "ingenious" was called an "engine." An ingenious weapon was called an engine of war. Most of the old war engines have gone out of use, except the gun, which we no longer call an engine. The bottling up of an expanding gas inside a tight jacket is the basic idea that makes most engines work—engines in the modern sense of the word. The force does not always have to be turned into circular motion by means of connecting rods and other such devices.

The first widely used engine which employed an expanding gas inside a tight jacket was the gun. Powerful guns on shipboard so changed the tricks of naval warfare that ships had to be built in a better way, to make them less vulnerable as targets.

Oars went out of use partly because ships needed more solidly built sides to withstand cannon shot, partly because galley slaves were too easily injured from a distance by the new "ingenious" weapon: the naval gun. Although the disadvantages were about the same on both sides for a time, the state of affairs was unsatisfactory to all naval powers. With both sides strong on the offensive and weak on the

defensive, there was a tendency for ships merely to cripple each other and drift apart.

In order to get real advantage from their new weapon or engine, navies in the early Fifteen Hundreds were driven to improve their ships, which became lower, stronger, and faster. After that had been accomplished, mainly by the Dutch and English, no very important changes occurred in naval architecture for the next two centuries.

Late in the Sixteen Hundreds, experiments were begun with the idea of putting the explosive power of steam to practical use by bottling it up in metal jackets. A little later, in 1736, Jonathan Hulls had progressed so far with the idea that he was able to patent a kind of "steam" boat which he described as a "New-Invented Machine for Carrying Vessels or Ships out of or into any harbor, port or river, against wind and tide or in a calm." From his own words it is very evident that Hulls thought of his steamboat strictly as a tug, to be used when sails were inconvenient or powerless because of the narrowness of a channel or the behavior of the wind. It is useful to remember this, because for more than a century after Jonathan Hulls' experiments, steam was thought of as something to help sails along in the pinches—just as sails, at an earlier period, were used as an assistance to the rowers, who provided the principal motive power.

Robert Fulton's steamboat of 1807, like the Wright brothers' airplane, was far from being the first of its kind. Fulton himself frankly admitted in his letters that he had not invented anything of great importance. His brand of genius, something like Donald McKay's, was concerned with making other men's ideas foolproof. His *Clermont* was the first steamboat that proved to be a paying proposition. But even when dozens of others quickly made use of the sound combination of principles evolved by Fulton, nobody believed that the days of sail were over. The *Clermont* carried some sails, and set them whenever there was any advantage to be got from them.

On the rivers of America, where there seldom was enough room in the narrow channels to use sails to advantage, steamers soon were appearing that had no sails at all. But in the open ocean, sails continued for many decades to be the more important kind of propeller.

THE "CLERMONT," LAUNCHED 1807

All through the period of slow change from sail to steam, and even up to the present day, vessels propelled by the wind alone have continued to be profitable freight carriers in some trades—notably in the transporting of lumber and grain.

Hence there is little evidence to support a claim, sometimes made, that the clipper-ship era was a final, superb answer made by sailing-ship men to the challenge of steam. Deep-water steamers still were half sailing ships long after the clippers as a type had vanished from the oceans. The American clipper-ship era ended a few years before our

THE "GREAT WESTERN," LAUNCHED 1838

Civil War began. It was not until 23 years after the war was over that the first ocean steamship appeared which was capable of traveling as fast as the *Sovereign of the Seas* had traveled in her great run in March, 1853.

Under favorable conditions the best sailing ships were speedier than the best steamships both before and during the clipper-ship era. Sail held the speed records for the fastest hour's and day's run for thirty years after the last clipper was launched.

What matters is that two good kinds of ships were being used at the same time, throughout the Eighteen Hundreds, each influencing the development of the other. During the earlier part of the century, sail alone dominated the ocean routes and steam alone came to dominate the rivers. At mid-century, steam *with the aid of sail in the same vessel* was putting up a stiff fight for the ocean trade, but the pure sailing ship was more than holding its own. Toward the end of the century, the *combination* of sail and steam gradually won out over the ship with sails alone, in most

THE "GREAT EASTERN," LAUNCHED 1858

trades. It was not until the late Eighteen Eighties that the honest race between sail and steam even began, because it was not until then that ocean steamers began to be built without provision for carrying any sails at all. By that time, the clipper as a class had vanished. It was not the threat of fast steamships that spurred the sailing ship men to super-human endeavors. But the use of the steam engine did make men aware of speed, and while some of them dreamt of the idea of fast steamships, the more practical ones turned their attention to the job of making fast sailing ships.

For thousands of years racehorses had provided the fastest means of travel. The use of steam on railways made it possible for the first time, about 1840, for men to travel faster than 35 miles an hour, the speed of a racing horse. This was an entirely new and wonderful idea in the practical world. In factories, the power of steam similarly upset the age-old notion of production, which had been limited to the strength and quickness of human hands. On the water, the steam engine gave sailors two entirely new ideas: they were no longer fated to sit and whistle for a wind when none was blowing, or to tack slowly back and forth against a directly contrary wind. Steam, at sea, did not at first mean sailing at a faster rate: it meant the chance to progress continuously, and in a straight line.

With the Industrial Revolution speeding up all the processes of making and of carrying the things men buy and sell, it was inevitable that the most widely used ma-chine in the world—the sailing ship—would feel the effect of the same process of improvement. Naval architects set about the job of improving it in that spirit. They could not have been driven to it by the idea that steamers were better, because for many years this was not true.

There are two ways of getting the kind of knowledge that goes into the improvement of things: the inspirational method and the experimental method. It is easier to think of them as the method of "dreaming" and the method of "try-it-and-see." The greatest inventions and developments came from a combination of both ways.

One kind of inventor gets an idea—dreams it—and tests it with mathematical formulas before he actually tries it out. The other kind of inventor makes a model, tinkers with it, discovers what may be wrong by watching the way it behaves. Then he changes it and tries it again. The change may make it worse instead of better. If so, he tries the opposite thing. Trial and error.

Astronomy gives us clear examples of these two ways of attacking the same kind of problem. And because celestial navigation has played a very important part in the use of our clipper ships of ocean and air, it is a proper example in any such story as this one. The theoretical astronomer may work for years without going near a telescope, spending his time instead on the job of trying to make sense out of other men's reports. The practical astronomer keeps his eye cocked at a lens and takes notes or photographs of just what he sees. A perfect instance of the way in which the two kinds of astronomers work together was revealed a few years ago in the identification of the ninth planet, Pluto. This tiny blob of light was really discovered by Percival Lowell, who never even saw it.

When C. W. Tombaugh, the first man who actually did see Pluto, picked it up with his telescope, Lowell had been dead for fourteen years. Yet Tombaugh found the faint, new speck just about where Lowell had said it would be. Lowell had computed its path mathematically because he observed other planets sometimes altering their orbits a trifle in a way that could be explained only by the pull of gravity from another heavenly body following a path where none had ever been seen.

Tombaugh at last found it on a photographic plate: a fleck of light among thousands of other similar ones that were distant stars. But this single fleck, lost among all the others, seemed to have changed its position slightly from the point where it had appeared on an earlier plate taken of the same part of the sky, in the constellation of Cancer. Tombaugh then kept his telescope trained on it night after night, taking more pictures to prove that it was continuing to move across the field of the true fixed stars in the direction, and at the speed, predicted by a man who had never seen it and who was fourteen years dead.

An astronomer had "dreamt" a new planet into existence in the sky by pure faith and the logic of mathematics. Another astronomer at last found it and identified it many years later, by the opposite patient method of "try-it-and-see."

When the Industrial Revolution turned the dream of speed toward the improvement of sailing ships, both the dreamers and the triers shared in the task. Both sorts of ship designers deserve credit for the result, and no single person can fairly be given the principal credit as inventor of the clipper ship. But if I were asked to make a choice between the two kinds of contributors to the process, I should have to choose the dreamers as being the more important.

The trial-and-error builders had been at work from a misty, forgotten day in the dawn of humanity when a first savage conceived the idea of crossing water by sitting astride a log and paddling with his hands. After that beginning, trial-and-error methods had muddled along for thousands of years, making many little improvements and some big ones. But what still was wanted, as the Eighteen Thirties came to a close, was a mathematically and physically correct dream of what a ship really should be: one based on true scientific principles rather than on luck.

To make that dream possible and necessary, a young nation first had to fall in love with the idea of speed. It found in the use of speed a means of competing with those who formerly had controlled the world's trade. The dreamers were hard-headed businessmen, as it happened, dreaming of the perfect ship for the frank reason that it would be a better money-maker. But that feature of the explanation has been overemphasized. It can be used just as well to explain the other side of the story. Hard-headed businessmen who wanted to be sure of their profits were the very ones who had called for the building of the worst and slowest ships of recent times, and the most dangerous. They had done so because certain peculiarities of the laws that provided for the taxation of vessels made it seem less expensive to own a bad ship than a good one.

Out of the many plans that were put forward for the improvement of ship design in the early Eighteen Forties, two quite different ones were thought good enough to merit a trial. That meant that someone with a lot of money would have to risk thirty or forty thousand dollars in building a ship on each of the two plans before their merits could be tested. Such a gamble was not likely to be taken in countries that had all the advantages of trade already. But an occasional merchant in a young country, struggling for what it considered to be its rightful share of the business of the world, was willing to assume the risk. The merchant himself had to be a gambler, which is to say, a dreamer of sorts. The first plan which found a merchant willing to back it was that of a practical, try-it-and-see seaman. The second plan, the one evolved by the dreamer-mathematician, waited a little longer for a sponsor to come forward.

After eight or ten years a third genius appeared, a very young genius, who experimented with combinations of the two schools of design. Soon afterward came the greatest genius of all, to shape and harmonize the ideas of his predecessors into a whole fleet of incomparably wonderful ships: a dozen or so that were all as good as any which ever have been built by other shipwrights, and half a dozen more which were so near to perfection that not one of them ever has been equaled by the combined efforts of all the other shipyards in the world.

The clipper-ship era produced other builders perhaps as important, but the achievements of these four men and of their ships can give us the main pattern of the achievements of the others as well. The two different basic ideas for improving speed were contributed, one by the practical shipmaster N. B. Palmer, the other by the draftsman J. W. Griffiths. The proper way in which to blend their different theories was realized by a youngster named S. H. Pook, first of the independent marine architects. Finally, the labors of all three were brought to perfection at last by a man who took pride in calling himself merely a "mechanic"—the ultimate genius of wooden ship building: Donald McKay.

The particular wave of progress which these four men brought to a swift, triumphant crest at mid-century had been set in motion by political occurrences seventy-five years earlier. If we are to understand how that wave rolled up to its spectacular triumph, we should go back and follow it from the beginning. And to get a clear view of what lies behind such processes, we should first take a quick glance at some accomplishments of even earlier days on the shores of the North Sea.

CHAPTER SIX

Nearly all early vessels of which reliable pictures survive were equipped with a single large square sail. "Square sail" is a phrase which refers less to the shape of the sails themselves than to the fact that the yards to which they are bent are set squarely across the mast, and are supported in the middle.

A single large square sail is cumbersome to handle and dangerous in a squall. It also draws poorly if the wind comes from a slanting direction. The whole sail will ripple and flap when the edge toward which the wind blows is not kept taut by some special device. Even the bowlines, which steadied the forward edges of square sails in the old days, were not satisfactory and were given up before the clippers came.

To get rid of this trouble, some early seaman hit upon the simple device of supporting his sail slantwise and off center. Most of the wind then encountered the rigid upper spar as a "leading edge," and only a minor part of it hit the luff or forward edge of sailcloth alone. Vessels so rigged were found in the East Indies, by early European explorers. But at a far earlier period someone in the Mediterranean region carried the idea to its sensible limit by pinching the forward ends of the two transverse spars completely together and spreading the after ends. The lower spar was presently eliminated, and the result was the lateen rig.

Lateen sails have been popular in the Mediterranean region from the Dark Ages, and are seen frequently still. They are efficient and easy to handle when the wind is abeam or ahead. But in "running free" with the wind astern the lateen is tricky and dangerous because of its extreme lopsidedness. Nevertheless, it had replaced square sail almost entirely by the time the naval gun first came into use.

The next great improvement in the mechanical principle of making sails more efficient as "engines," or "ingenious" devices for propulsion, took place on the Netherlands coasts. This was early in the Fifteen Hundreds, when the rebel Dutch began the century of bitter warfare that at last freed them from Spanish tyranny. The Netherlands were blockaded, off and on, by strong fleets equipped with naval guns that may well have seemed invincible. But the Dutch, wherever they could possess themselves of a little coastal land and defend it, began to build vessels of a new sort, smaller yet swifter than the galleasses or the somewhat later galleons of Spain. They displayed the typical ingenuity to which men are driven by the very fact of tyranny itself.

The best ships of the Fourteen Hundreds had almost given up square sail in favor of as many as four lateen sails, each on its separate mast. But some of the advantages of the lateen sail were lost when too many of them were used together. With the development of castles fore and aft, and the complicated rig needed to support several masts, the lateen triangles became taller, and shorter at the base.

Then, as heavier guns came into use in greater numbers for each vessel, the added weight and strength of construction made the tall triangular sails seem inadequate, because they filled only a diagonal lower half of the space available. The swing back to square sails began. By making them less broad and using more of them, with separate "top" sails above the "main" sails, it was possible to fill the spaces between the closely set masts more efficiently. More power was attained to move the heavier weights of guns and thick bulwarks, but at a sacrifice of maneuvering qualities. Square sails were better for running before the wind, but not as good as lateen sails for tacking against it.

The typical large ship of war of the early Fifteen Hundreds had some of each, carrying square sail on the fore and main masts, with lateen sails on the two after masts. Perhaps it was some particular forgotten Dutchman, looking grimly and critically at one of those early galleons, who saw what was wrong. When the wind was coming from ahead the lateen sails could have been trimmed still to catch and use it after the square sails had been taken aback. Yet at that very moment the wider and clumsier square sails

PRE-CHRISTIAN

MEDIEVAL

1520

1570

1720

THE EVOLUTION OF SAIL

1820

would begin to cut the lateen sails off from a headwind. Moreover, the lack of spars to keep the lower edges of any but the topsails taut and steady wasted a lot of power.

It cannot be proved by existing evidence that anyone ever sat down, drew a triangular sail across a mast, added a boom to stiffen the foot of it, and then cut free the portion forward of the mast to form a jib. But that is what history finally did to the lateen rig.

The rig was further developed and refined by making the main sail taller and splitting the jib into two or more separate headsails, but the device had been discovered by which the forward edges of all the sails could be kept from shivering—the headsails on the taut rope stays leading from the mast head to the bow or bowsprit, and the mainsail by being laced or parreled to the mast itself.

The basis for this ultimate arrangement of fore-and-aft sails was among the many Dutch contributions to naval architecture in the Fifteen Hundreds. Faced by fleets that had been built originally for the different sailing conditions of the Mediterranean and middle Atlantic regions, the Dutch set to work to change and improve the designs of hulls as well as sails. In this they had one main object: to keep out of range of the Spanish cannon. They accomplished their object in two ways: by making ships that would sail well under all conditions with the wind from any quarter, and by making them quickly maneuverable. Having done these two things, their fewer ships did not have to give battle except when conditions seemed favorable. Gradually, in a series of actions, they broke the Spanish power.

Across the channel the English were watching. They

bought Dutch ships for their own navy, and then copied their good points. When Spain turned for a while from the Netherlands, and made a last great try at northern domination by sending the "Invincible Armada" toward England, the English had learnt the Dutch lesson well. The Armada was destroyed partly by weather, partly by brilliant English seamanship, partly by the good Dutch-taught design of English ships. But all three of those advantages which the smaller fleet had over the larger one can be charged back to the tyrant, Philip of Spain. He counted on the tyranny of numbers, and so used ships that were not as well designed as they might have been to face the storms of northern waters, or the quick handling of the more weatherly Dutch-inspired ships of England.

The fate of the Armada decided the question of maritime supremacy so far as Spain was concerned. The struggle thereafter was between the English and the Dutch—and again the older sea power succumbed to the younger one. The Dutch were supreme at sea until about 1670 when, largely as a result of the work of the diarist Pepys, the British navy became the most powerful single national fleet in the world.

And then the old story renewed itself. As the British navy increased in quantity and in size of ships, the desperate need for improvement no longer was felt. It was more convenient to standardize everything, to divide ships into various "rates" according to their importance as measured by the number of guns they could carry. Tradition—always a strong force at sea—took possession of the service. It became almost a heresy to suggest new ideas. As one example of this conservatism, the basic specifications for guns and gun carriages in the British navy showed no essential changes for two hundred years, from the time of Henry VIII.

For a period of similar length, beginning in the days of Queen Elizabeth, there were no very notable improvements of any kind in naval architecture. The forecastles had disappeared before that. Little by little, the aftercastles were reduced. The bowsprit, which had begun as a kind of tilted mast to steady the other masts, was first given a square sprit sail and was thereafter gradually lowered and lengthened until the Dutchman's inventions—headsails—were put where they belonged.

The galleon sail plan, with triangular lateen sails aft, gave way to a final development used to the end in large sailing ships. The after part of the lateen sail survived on the mizzen in the form of a spanker, and the fore parts of two or more lateen sails were put up forward where they would do most good, on a bowsprit that steeved less sharply upward.

Some refinements were made in the form of the hull and the mechanism of the rudder, but nothing very vital was done. That was because no very vital need for improvement was felt until, after a century or more of unquestioned British domination on the ocean, two other peoples began to find tyranny unendurable, and to cast about for every possible means of freeing themselves.

Historians are still arguing as to whether the French or the Americans were chiefly responsible for the new wave of progress in ship design that began in the Seventeen Seventies. From our point of view, in the United States, it hardly matters. No-one who has taken the trouble to study the

1620

1780

evidence has denied that America continued the improvement at an ever increasing pace until, with a final miraculous burst of genius and enterprise, the shipbuilders of New York and New England circled the world with the Yankee Clippers: a great fleet of sailing ships, faster and more beautiful than those built in any other nation, before or since.

CHAPTER SEVEN

THE SPANISH BLOCKADES OF THE NETHERLANDS COAST perhaps should not be called by that name, which probably was not invented until they were over. A blockade is a declaration stating the conditions under which neutral ships will be allowed to trade with the blockader's enemy. If it is a bluff that cannot really be enforced, it is called a "paper blockade." A blockade generally aims to prevent all ships from entering or leaving any enemy port. It further provides that neutral ships which do not obey the blockade orders will be treated as if they were enemies: captured or sunk.

The success of a blockade depends largely upon the geographical character of the coasts and ports concerned.

One strategic little American port, now almost forgotten, is so located that it has played a large part in two blockades. As it is also the birthplace of one of the famous designers of clipper ships, N. B. Palmer, it is a good point upon which to focus a study of the actual effects of blockade upon progress in ship design.

The stretch of water about fifteen miles wide between Montauk and Stonington—the port in question—forms the outer bottle neck of Long Island Sound. The Sound's other entrance, at Hell Gate, was so narrow and shallow in Nat Palmer's youth—before the reefs were blasted out—that sizable vessels seldom attempted to get through. As a consequence, nearly all the commerce to and from other parts of the Sound sailed past Stonington. Hell Gate, dangerous in any case, could be made completely impassable if a few cannon were mounted on shore. A small blockading squadron, reaching to and fro between Stonington and Montauk, could make it extremely difficult for merchantmen to get into and out of the ports situated on Long Island's north shore and on Connecticut's rivers and coast. Great Britain, when the American Revolution began, turned these facts promptly to account.

On the 25th of July, 1775, five weeks after the battle of Bunker Hill, the British men-of-war *Rose*, *Swan*, and *Kingfisher* appeared off New London to announce a blockade. On the 30th of August, Sir James Wallace in the *Rose* chased a small vessel inside Fisher's Island and sent an armed boat from the frigate to capture her when she sought shelter at the Stonington wharf. The local militia beat the boat off, whereupon Captain Wallace let go with round shot and cannonaded the village.

The only casualty was one man wounded, but the affair rankled in the memory of Stonington. Ships going into or out of the Sound had always regarded the place as a good anchorage at which to refit, or to take in provisions, or to recruit excellent seamen. Blockade ruined the port's principal reason for existence. An old history of near-by New London says, in describing those days, "While the enemy thus kept possession of the Sound, the sloops and boats belonging to the coast, melted away like summer snow." The historian adds that the blockaders were diligently "destroying coasters and fishing vessels without mercy."

The boys of Nat Palmer's world, a generation later, could see the round shot that had been picked up as souvenirs of the *Rose's* attack, and hear stories from veteran sailors about the little blockade runners and privateers that were the best answers the Connecticut Yankees could make to the big British ships and guns.

When George Washington's army lost the battle of Long Island, the never very useful Hell Gate passage out of the Sound became completely useless to the Americans. Blockade runners could creep along most of the American coast, dodging into harbor when necessary, to lie under the guns of a friendly fort. But as soon as the south shore of Long Island was taken over by the British, there was a long dangerous gap in the series of such sanctuaries. Here then was where the big gamble occurred, whenever a coaster tried to run between Massachusetts and the southerly colonies.

The most perilous job of all was to try to get out of any Connecticut port, past the blockaders off Stonington, then to stand southwestward down the hostile Long Island coast that afforded no shelter for a Yankee, and finally through or around a second British squadron on Sandy Hook station.

That double blockade was so effective in disrupting the coastal communications of the Americans that it greatly prolonged the Revolution. Yet the ultimate effects may have been more harmful to England than helpful—for the tactics of blockade drove the Connecticut Yankees to design sailing craft of a sort able to cope with the situation. The builders of the successful blockade-runners developed a tradition in marine architecture which soon was producing peaceful ships to capture—before 1855—the larger part of England's most profitable world trade.

But first a series of severe setbacks drove home the absolute necessity for finding new principles. Connecticut's navy consisted of eleven small craft and two modest ships. The largest vessel was only 80 feet in length, and carried about 20 guns. She could not engage frigates twice her size, to say nothing of the British 74's. It was useless to try to break the blockade. The Connecticut navy could merely retaliate against enemy supply ships and small armed craft.

The state began to build three fighting ships for the Continental Navy. One of them was not yet finished when the war ended. The other two were the small frigates *Trumbull* of 36 guns and *Confederacy* of 32. In an effort to get something quickly into service, ships had been authorized that were not quite adequate. Either one would have been knocked to splinters in no time by the main ships of the blockading squadron. Even the ordinary British frigates were more heavily armed than they were. The two little Continental frigates thus were as useless as the Connecticut navy in any effort to break the blockade. Both managed to dodge out successfully, but they were soon tracked down and captured at sea.

In a third effort, the Continental Congress authorized some 74-gun ships which would have been big enough to tackle the major blockaders. This decision came too late. Materials and equipment had been foolishly used up in the earlier building program. It proved impossible to finish any of the 74's while the war continued.

In the meanwhile, self-reliant Connecticut Yankees began to experiment with unarmed cargo carriers built entirely for speed and weatherliness, to knife around the edges of the blockades. They put small privateers in the water, differing from the traditional sea plunderers in that no attempt was made to equip them for long cruises or for defense against war vessels of comparable size. They were strong enough to capture supply ships and to keep armed cutters at bay, but they too had their main advantages in speed and weatherliness. They could outwit the largest ships by standing to windward at a sharper angle than was possible for a heavily built man-of-war, and they could evade smaller enemies by quick maneuvering in shallow channels.

Many of the vessels captured by Connecticut privateers had but recently been taken from American owners by the blockaders, who had sent them with small prize crews toward New York or Nova Scotia. But these captives were just as valuable to the privateersmen as if they had always belonged to the enemy. The law courts of both countries ruled that the claims of the original owners of a vessel ended when she was taken by any properly commissioned naval vessel or privateer. Thus, if the British captured a sloop belonging to Mr Pendleton of Stonington, and the sloop was recaptured five minutes later by a privateer belonging to Nat Palmer's father, also of Stonington, Mr Pendleton would have no legal claim to recover his former property from his neighbor.

This was understood on all sides, and was one reason for the common practice of splitting up the ownership of both unarmed vessels and privateers into shares. Thirty-two different men might combine to divide the risk of ownership. A man who lost his share in a vessel when she was taken by the British might regain it because he also owned a share in a privateer that recaptured her. The commonest arrangement was for two or three well-to-do men to own a majority of the thirty-two shares in such an enterprise, while six or eight other individuals held one or two shares apiece.

Shipyards were not very complicated in those days. A sloping stretch of firm shoreline, running down evenly into water deep enough to float the intended vessel, was about all that was needed. The proprietors of the yard had a saw pit dug, and supplied the two-man saws and the heavy mallets called mauls. Practically all of the other tools were owned by the individual ship carpenters. In most cases these included only ax, adz, auger, and plumb line—sometimes with the addition of chisels, hand saws, planes, and squares.

Such simplicity of equipment made it easy to hide a Connecticut shipyard anywhere beyond the first bend of every sizable stream. Slowly at first, then with increasing success, the workers in these yards found ways of bettering their products. The first great advance was one that seems obvious to us now. They made the individual vessels longer and narrower. Generally, in the Seventeen Hundreds, a proportion of about three to one was considered correct for small craft. More than fifty years after the American Revolution was over, designers for the British navy seldom had increased the percentage beyond three-and-a-half to one. R. H. Dana, Jr, in *The Seaman's Friend,* quotes statistics for the year 1841 to show that typical British men-of-war were only 3.16 times as long as they were wide, when merchant vessels—supposedly a slower class of ships—already were commonly given a proportion in America of about 4.6 to 1. That proportion was to increase further, very rapidly, in the next decade or so, until a ration of 5.7 to 1 was reached in the extreme clippers.

It seems only common sense to say that the longer a ship was, the less she would slip sidewise and the faster she would move forward, given the same amount of power. But the solution of the problem was not quite as easy as that.

Those who argued for the 3 to 1 ratio pointed out that a ship must be "stiff" in order to use the wind's power effectively. If she were heeled over at a 45° angle because she had been made narrower and thus easier to upset, the amount of wind she actually would catch would be reduced just as much as if the yards themselves were braced around at a 45° angle from the most effective and efficient one.

A longer, narrower ship would stow less cargo for the amount that she cost to build, and would be less strong in dangerous weather. And there were other arguments.

The answer, as in most such cases, was not to choose one thing or the other, but to find a new basis or principle which would reassure both sides. If vessels were to be made longer and narrower, then they also must be made stronger by improved methods of construction, and their center of gravity must be brought lower to compensate for the loss of breadth.

But the main driving force still was necessity itself. Circumstances, in all the little Connecticut yards, were similar to those of the days when the Dutch were throwing off Spanish tyranny. The side with weaker weapons but stronger will found new ways of succeeding. In comfortable times, when any standard vessel would earn a comfortable living, there was little incentive for risking money on new ideas. But under the blockade, when standard vessels were almost certain to be captured, a new idea was worth the gamble. If it did not work, the investor was no worse off than if he had done the standard thing. If it did work, he profited by it.

Other schemes were tried. A Connecticut man named David Bushnell even built a submarine, early in the Revolution, and also devised various kinds of mines and torpedoes which were used with some effect against the blockaders of the Sound. But the most useful contribution of the Connecticut Yankees in the long run proved to be their experimentation upon the shape and structure of sailing craft.

Young Nat Palmer's father, by turns a lawyer and shipbuilder, learnt the rudiments of the latter trade in those exacting days when there was only one hard rule to go by: an unsuccessful vessel was quickly captured, whereas a successful one slipped past the blockaders, again and again. A hesitant commander might lose a good vessel by bad management. A good commander might lose a humdrum craft even while he was getting all the speed out of her that any-one humanly could. But when any commander brought the same vessel through the blockade several times, the builders were justified in assuming that her shape had a lot to do with it.

A captain might report that the narrow, fishtail lines given his new sloop expressly for speed seemed instead to make her drag and settle aft. Such practical negative re-ports would be borne in mind in designing the next sloop, which would be a little more buoyant in the after body.

Records are scanty to show the exact course of experi-mentation. Hints in the local newspapers, and even more revealing letters by British officers who had chased such small craft unsuccessfully, provide some information. But one circumstance tells more than volumes of exact plans. This is the later and highly detailed account which we do possess of the shipbuilding achievements of the great Con-necticut-trained men of the next generation or two. It is certainly more than a coincidence that a majority of the most famous New York builders of packet ships and clip-pers were men who had migrated down the coast from Connecticut, where they had served their apprenticeships under resourceful old codgers who had developed the blockade-runners of the Revolution.

The shipbuilder who contributed more than any other man to our naval victories in the War of 1812 lived on an-other stretch of coast that had been closely blockaded in the Revolution. His name was Joshua Humphreys. For years he argued with our legislators in an attempt to explain the right principles for building better frigates. Even a casual rereading of his arguments is enough to prove that he was thinking in terms of blockade.

The final large confirmation of the effect of blockades on ship design is to be found in the records of the famous Baltimore clippers, which throughout the early Eighteen Hundreds were freely acknowledged to be the fastest things afloat. Baltimore, in the throat of blockaded Chesapeake Bay—Philadelphia up the blockaded Delaware River—Connecticut on blockaded Long Island Sound: these were the three locations of the most severe and continuous blockades of the Revolution—and between them they wrote nearly the whole story of the advancement in naval architecture that came in the days of "try-it-and-see." Even afterward, when great theoretical designers brought the science to the very edge of perfection itself, they proved to be men trained under five Connecticut masters, Adam and Noah Brown, Jacob Bell, Stephen Smith, and Isaac Webb.

John W. Griffiths worked for Stephen Smith. Donald McKay was taught his art by Isaac Webb, and practiced it for Brown and Bell. N. B. Palmer also worked with the Browns and with Bell in designing the first two clippers he commanded.

CHAPTER EIGHT

THE SOCIETY OF FRIENDS, CALLED QUAKERS BY MOST people, is opposed to war on principle. In wartime, the Friends do what they can to relieve suffering, but the conscientious ones will have nothing to do with fighting. It is curious that the father of the American navy should have been of Welsh Quaker descent, a practicing Friend himself until a committee of the society "read him out of meeting" for his entirely too obvious contributions to the weapons of the Revolution.

Joshua Humphreys was born on June 17th, 1751, near the present site of Haverford College in Pennsylvania. He was early apprenticed to a shipbuilder named Penrose, who died before the apprenticeship was completed. The shipbuilder's widow released the apprentice from the terms of the agreement. An unfinished ship was on the stocks at the time. Joshua Humphreys completed the vessel so satisfactorily that he continued in charge of the Penrose yard. Before he came of age, he joined with his cousin John Wharton in the construction of several vessels. He also built a "galley" to help defend the city of Philadelphia.

When Humphreys was twenty-four years old, the new Continental Congress authorized the construction of thirteen cruisers, and the reputation of the firm of Wharton and Humphreys was already sufficient to get them the appointment to build one of the ships. They lost no time. Their ship, the frigate *Randolph*, 32 guns, got to sea early in 1777.

A young builder would have watched closely the news of his first fighting vessel's career. The fate of the *Randolph* undoubtedly made a deep impression upon Humphreys. In building her, Wharton and Humphreys seem to have produced precisely what the government ordered, as a sister ship of identical dimensions was built in another yard. But the same lack of foresight that made the Connecticut-built warships of the Continental Navy a failure became evident even earlier in the case of the *Randolph*. She was about as small as a ship could be, to deserve the frigate rating: 126 feet, 3½ inches long; 34 feet, 10 inches beam. Her earliest encounters were successful, when she captured four Jamaica vessels, of which the most notable mounted 20 guns.

Captain Biddle got his four prizes safely into Charleston, South Carolina, but news of his exploits traveled quickly, and he found himself blockaded there by British cruisers of superior force. After the better part of a year of helpless idling, he was given command of a fleet of four additional vessels commissioned by the State of South Carolina. Accompanied by these, he made a run for it.

The British ship of the line *Yarmouth* was waiting for him, carrying exactly twice as many guns as were mounted by the *Randolph*. The American frigate could neither outsail nor outshoot her big enemy. While the smaller North Carolina vessels scattered for safety, Humphreys' ship went into action. She stood the terrific pounding for twenty minutes, until a hot shot entered her powder magazine and she was blown to bits; 311 members of her crew of 315 were killed.

Joshua Humphreys in the meanwhile had fitted out the fleet of eight vessels, all even smaller than the *Randolph*, which put to sea under Commodore Esek Hopkins. The navy's first commodore had better success than Captain Biddle, made possible by the good luck of meeting no enemy ships which could not either be beaten because they were weaker or left behind because they were slower.

Despite the plans of the government and the best efforts of such men as Humphreys, it proved impossible to produce an effective navy while the war was in progress. The ships which would have been big enough to lift the blockades were never finished. The ones that were finished proved too small. Privateers were generally successful, but the only really notable sea fight from the official American navy's point of view—that against the *Serapis*—was fought by John Paul Jones in a ship provided by the French.

When the war was over, the United States thought that a peacefully intended nation ought to be able to get along without a navy, and managed to do so for ten increasingly difficult years. Some members of the government were what we nowadays would call appeasers. They believed that in the long run it would produce less suffering to give other countries what they demanded, and that the cost of doing so would be no greater than the cost of enforcing American rights by fighting for them.

The noisiest international gangsters of those days were the Barbary States. They thought of their waters as being a kind of international toll-highway of the sea. Ships that wanted to use that highway should pay for the privilege. Otherwise they were subject to capture. The Barbary pirates preferred to call themselves corsairs, and Moslem boys became sea raiders as naturally as young men today might go into the police force or revenue service. The corsairs, from their own point of view, were a sort of combination of both.

In 1796, when most of the French commissioners with whom Charles Pinckney was negotiating suggested that they would appreciate a substantial gift of money, he made his famous answer: "Millions for defense, sir, but not one cent for tribute." When he said it he should have known, as a responsible diplomat, that the appeasers in Congress a few months earlier had authorized a treaty with Algiers providing for the payment each year of tribute in maritime stores worth over $20,000.

Appeasement never works. No sooner was one of the four Barbary States bought off than another became jealous and troublesome. Apart from tribute paid meekly in accordance with signed treaties, the value of ships captured and of ransoms for enslaved crew members began to run into millions of dollars. In the fall of 1793 American vessels were being seized at a rate of two a week.

Even before that, Joshua Humphreys had become so perturbed about the defenseless condition of the country that he had sent a letter to Robert Morris, senator from Pennsylvania, urging action. Despite the fact that it came from a private citizen, it is one of the most important letters on naval affairs ever written. It contains a basic idea, so quietly and simply stated that the casual reader might miss its importance. Yet it is hardly too much to say that if Joshua Humphreys had not been on hand to write a letter to his senator on January 6th, 1793, the United States very probably would have been so disastrously defeated in the war which came twenty years later that it would have ceased to exist as an independent nation. Here is the letter:

Southwark Jany 6. 1793

Robert Morris Esq.

Sir

From the present appearance of affairs, I believe it is time this country was possesed of a Navy; but as that is yet to be raised, I have ventured a few Ideas on that subjet.

Ships that compose the European navys are generally distinguished by their rates; but as the situations and depth of Water of our coasts & Harbours are different in some degree from those in Europe, & as our Navy must for a considerable time be inferior in numbers we are to consider what size Ships will be most formidable and be an over match for those of an Enemy, such Frigates as in blowing weather as would be an over match for double deck Ships, & in light winds, to evade coming to action, or double deck Ships as would be an over match for common double deck Ships, and in blowing weather superior to Ships of three Decks, or in calm weather or light winds to out-sail them. Ships built on these principles will render those of an Enemy in a degree useless, or require a greater number before they dare attack our Ships.

Frigates I suppose will be the first object and none ought to be built less than 150 feet keel to carry 28, 32 pounders or 30, 24 pounders on the main gun deck & 12 pounders on the quarter deck. Those ships should have scantling equal to 74rs—and I believe may be built of Red cedar & Live Oak for about twenty four pounds ℔ Ton Carpenter tonage including, Carpenters bill, Smith, including Anchors, Joyners, Boat builders, Painters, Plumbers, Carvers, Coopers, Block makers, Mast Makers, Riggers & Rigging, sail makers & sail cloth two suits & chandlers bill.

As Such Ships will cost a large sum of money they should be built of the best materials, that could possibly be procured, the beams for their decks should be of the best Carolina pine & the lower Futtocks & Knees if possible of Live Oak. The greatest care should be taken in the construction of such Ships, and particularly all her timbers should be Framed and bolted together before they are raised.

Frigates built to carry 12, 18 pounders in my opinion will not answer the expectation contemplated from them, for if we should be obliged to take a part in the present European War, or at a future day, we should be dragged into a War with any powers of the old continent, especially great Britain they having such a number of Ships of that Size, that it would be an equal chance by equal combat that we loose our Ships and more particularly from the Algerien, who have Ships & some of much greater force. several questions will arise, whether will one large or two small Frigates contribute most to the protection of our trade or which will cost the least sum of money, or whether two small ones are as able to engage a double deck ship as one large one. for my part I am decidedly of opinion, the large ones will answer best.

I am very Respectfully

JOSHUA HUMPHREYS

In those words of Humphreys' are summed up the particular kind of enterprise which was applied increasingly for the next sixty years on the American coasts, to make the United States for a little while the most important maritime nation in the world. It was the principle of questioning every old tradition, of thinking things down to a basic idea and starting afresh.

For centuries the older, wealthier countries had been building up their fleets, adding more single powerful ships as the best means of outclassing the enemy.

This kind of competition, before 1800, had given the major navies many ships carrying more than 100 guns apiece. These were called "first rates." The expression "first rate" remains in our language to remind us of ships that exist no longer. Second rates carried 90 or more guns, third rates were usually 74's, and fourth rates had about 56.

All of these were "ship rigged"—had three masts carrying square sail.

That has been for nearly three centuries the strict definition of the word "ship." It now means any steam- or oil-propelled vessel of moderate size or larger. But many seamen still are scornful of anyone who uses the word "ship" in reference to a type, however large, that has a proper name of its own. Some schooners and barks have been much larger than the average ship-rigged vessel. But nothing, to an old salt, is a ship unless it has either no sails whatever or else crosses squaresail on each of three masts.

Fighting ships were further classified by their number of decks. First and second rates had three gun-decks, third and fourth rates had two. H M S Victory, Nelson's flagship and the most famous of all first rates, is still preserved in England. It looks almost like a floating fortress, old style, with high sides necessary to provide so many gun ports in three tiers, and great width to steady her under the shock of letting go a broadside.

Line-of-battle ships (74's and larger) were so called because they were intended to go into action in the main line of a fleet, while smaller and swifter ones ranged on one flank or both.

When other aspects of design are equal, the maximum speed of ships increases with their size. The big first rates were slower mainly because they were so heavily built and armed. The smallest vessels of the fleet also were comparatively slow: they could not stand up under as great a proportion of sail. Between these two classes, and protecting both, ranged the frigates, big enough to gain the speed which comes of size, and armed as well as any ship needed to be that could sail away from the enemy's heavy ships of the line. Frigates were ship-rigged single-deckers. They carried some guns on a slightly raised quarterdeck, but their main batteries were all in a single row.

Starting from scratch in a world of other navies that had existed for centuries, Joshua Humphreys knew it would be folly to begin to build up that line of battle either with the middle or with the edges. On the long coast of the United States actions between big fleets might never be called for. In the narrow waters of the seas around Europe, such as the English Channel or the Strait of Gibraltar, conditions had made it logical to pit fleet against fleet. What America wanted, as Humphreys saw it, was the kind of ship that could cruise alone: a ship neither too big nor too small: a frigate. From a solid basis of frigates to start off with, bigger and smaller vessels might follow later as the need arose. Also, the country was poor, and three or four frigates could be built for the cost of one first-rate.

That decision was only the beginning of the problem. The next thing Humphreys had to face (and it is something which the popular historians of the War of 1812 often overlook) is the fact that in almost all cases victory goes to the side with the heaviest total weight of guns and the most men. There are times when by superior courage and skill a little fellow comes off the victor, but Humphreys knew better than to count on it in building a navy from the very beginning. Beside ships of the line, each of the larger naval powers of his day had scores of frigates. He had been authorized to build six. Foreign frigates in some cases would be backed up by larger vessels. His would never be, at least for many years. In a series of single ship actions, the honors would probably be even. If he built six ordinary frigates, the mathematical chances were that only three would win their first fights. Against equal opponents, all of those would be due to lose their second ones. Thus nine actions would put an end to his navy. Moreover, if the bigger opponents should send their more numerous frigates cruising in pairs, the single American ships of the same size would always lose.

Far from believing in the myth which later romantic writers have built up, that one American rookie seaman was worth two of any other country, Humphreys actually wrote, ". . . if we . . . had ships of equal size with theirs, for want of experience and discipline, which cannot be immediately expected, in an engagement we should not have an equal chance, and probably lose our ships."

His plan, therefore, was to build frigates a little larger than any others afloat, to arm them with heavier guns than were carried by any old world frigates, and still to make them as strong and sharp as possible. All the experience of England and France had gone into the production of definite classes of ships. They had so many that it seemed foolish to build any that would be midway in size and strength between the standard single-deck 38-gun frigate and the smallest double-deck fourth-rate of 50 guns. If a one-decker would not do whatever job the Lords of the Admiralty had in mind, they sent out a two-decker. Having plenty of both, they saw no particular need for complicating the situation with yet another class.

But for America, starting with no navy at all, another class was precisely what was needed. Despite the objections of sensible men who dared not trust anything that had not been tried before, Humphreys convinced the bigwigs. Perhaps it was a good thing that there was as yet no official secretary of the navy. The man serving in place of one was (like our first World War II Secretary of the Navy in both name and experience) a former army officer called Knox. A naval man would probably have been less ready to gamble on the ideas of an ex-Quaker who had never been in either of the fighting services himself.

Six frigates were designed by Humphreys according to the principles he had so carefully explained. Against strong opposition, five of them were completed according to his plans. The sixth, the *Chesapeake*, was altered in the building by a subordinate named Fox. She alone, of Humphreys' six famous frigates, was defeated in a single-ship action.

After they were built, Humphreys stated his argument again, briefly, as follows: "They are superior to any European frigate, and if others should be in company, our frigates can always lead ahead and never be obliged to go into action, but on their own terms, except in a calm; in blowing weather our ships are capable of engaging to advantage double-deck ships."

Five of the new frigates soon were sent, together with smaller vessels, against the Barbary Corsairs. But as these activities had no influence upon the trend of ship design, there is no excuse for following the early careers of Humphreys' ships in the Mediterranean. While Americans, for a change, were blockading other people's coasts, another ship designer was having his first good look at the world in the port of Stonington.

CHAPTER NINE

"My home is here in Stonington," Captain Alexander Palmer is said to have remarked, "but Nat's home is the world."

It was the modest tribute of a fine sea captain to a great one who happened to be his elder brother. Both were globe-girdlers, again and again. But Nat Palmer did more than that. He saw his own name written on the most difficult edge of the map of the world when he was scarcely twenty-two years old, in recognition of the fact that a year earlier he had joined the extremely exclusive company of men who have discovered continents. Before he was forty, he added to his fame by contributing a vital new principle to the art of shipbuilding that made the development of the ultimate clippers more certain.

Imagine yourself in the world of about the year 1800, which Nat Palmer began to be aware of—with eyes and nose and hands—as his outlook expanded, first over the top-sides of a wooden cradle, then beyond the bulkheads of his nursery. It was a world in which the clean, acid smell of sawn Connecticut oak blew in on the west wind from the shipyards, mingled with the reek of seaweed drying crisp above the barnacles—a smell that came and went as the moon tugged the tides to and fro.

Horseshoe crabs lay on the mud flats at low tide, their spiky tails aloft. Clams were easier for a child to find than for his elders, because his eyes were nearer the tell-tale circle made by a wrinkled, collapsible black neck that could be hauled so quickly back into the shell.

In the fishing boats, the extra weight of a six-year-old might be considered worth while, for the sake of one more line held over the side by fingers that quickly learnt the difference between the insistent, quick twinges of a min-now worrying at the bait and the less definite but more important small tug when a real fish quietly took it into his jaws.

It was a world in which a boy, racing down to the wharves, was far more likely to dodge past a neighbor who last had set foot on the island of Java, twelve thousand miles away, than one who ever had journeyed inland one-fiftieth as far, to Buffalo. The rocky shore of Stonington Point was like a division between the easy open way of travel toward Portugal or China, and the hard route to such dismally remote villages as Pittsburgh and Cincinnati. The

sea in 1800, as it is now, was one broad highway, leading
everywhere. Sometimes it was angry, or tedious with contrary winds. But the land in those days seemed humped
and tedious always. When you think yourself back into Nat
Palmer's world, remember that it is the land that has
changed tremendously. Then it was scrawled over, here and
there, by a few rutted and boggy roads, seldom used except
for short distances. The main routes inland were up the
rivers. Water was the only sensible surface on which to
transport heavy loads of freight. For many years after 1800
men took it for granted that it made better sense to dig a
canal between two lowland cities than to build an adequate
road.

That was the state of affairs inland. Most Stonington
men turned their backs on such absurdities, and kept their
faces and imaginations toward the sea.

Down at the bonded warehouse, Uncle Jonathan Palmer
surveyed incoming vessels, received their cargoes, and assessed duties and tonnage fees. Young Nat knew that any
day he might find there, waiting for a berth, one of the
dozen or so of Stonington seamen who had sailed off round
the world in 1797 with Fanning, in the *Betsey*. They were
men who could be coaxed into telling spine-tingling tales
of Indians very different from the tame, unhappy Pequots
in the North Stonington reservation.

Even for satisfactory Indians, boys looked seaward in
those days. The word "Indian" still hung on to some of its
original meaning, for Americans of 1800. It meant a native
of the Indies—the East Indies which Columbus thought
he had found when he encountered somewhat similar islands in the Caribbean. The men of the *Betsey* called all

[85]

the native islanders of the South Pacific Indians too. They told of such notables as their friend Toohoorebooa and others who lived in a perplexing kind of paradise in the Marquesas Islands, where blue tattooing was worn instead of clothes, and where people beautiful as angels dined with great gusto on the succulent steamed arms and legs of neighbors who had displeased them.

The dirtily but respectably dressed Pequots at home were more sedate in their behavior.

More important to our present considerations, as we try to pick up the many trends which merged and aided one another in producing the clippers, is a different kind of story also brought home in the *Betsey*. All Stonington had heard it from Parson Avery's pulpit, as well as from the seamen who were so lucky as to have lived to tell it.

It was the story of the night when Captain Fanning, unable to sleep because of fears and doubts he could not explain, finally had come on deck to order the light sails in, the topsails single-reefed, and the brig brought to on a wind to await daylight. His officers had thought it queer, as there was no sign of danger, and no indication of it on the charts. But dawn revealed a line of tremendous breakers, stretching in a great crescent, with the wind blowing directly toward them.

The *Betsey* had already been put about in the darkness, pointing back as closely as she could be made to lie in the direction from which she had come. There was nothing to do but to hope that she could gain enough distance northward to weather the reef, before her leeway—the distance she was being blown sidewise—would drive her ashore.

One of Fanning's men, sketching in the sand with his

forefinger, could make it plain enough that a vessel would have to be "weatherly" to escape from such a situation. She would have to be able to use the leverage of her sails to convert the largest possible part of the force of the north-east trade wind into motive power that would push the brig northward, back somewhat against the wind itself. Seamen called a brig "weatherly" if she was comparatively long and narrow, permitting her yards to be braced up sharp. But no brig could compare with a fore-and-after at getting to windward.

In a case such as that of the *Betsey* caught on a lee shore, with the wind and probably the currents both tending to move her toward destruction, the problem is first to catch the force of the wind in sails, then to turn the force at an angle by pointing the yards sharply against the wind, and finally to use that force pushing on the mast fulcrums in such a way as to convert the whole ship into one big lever. The resulting lever does not have a solid fulcrum to work against. It slips sidewise, wasting more and more of the force of the sails the more closely it tries to reverse the actual direction from which the force is coming in the form of wind.

Captain Fanning, in his own account of the voyage of the *Betsey*, ends the story simply by saying that he sent an officer aloft to see whether the brig was nearer to the north or the south end of the reef, and whether they would be likely to clear it by remaining on the same tack. He ends, "We were so fortunate as to weather the breakers on our stretch to the north." But behind his simple statement lay just as complicated a calculation as an airplane pilot must make when he is flying blind across a pass in the Himalayas, knowing that he must compute his drift sidewise, his altitude compared with that of the pass, his speed, his experience of downward currents, and many lesser factors.

Practical seamen did most of their calculating, in such circumstances, by what they would have called instinct. But in using that word they meant more than you might think, because they insisted too that it was an officer's first duty to come "to know his ship." By trying her out, by experimenting with various amounts of sail under different circumstances, by using more or less of the "head sail" canvas forward of the foremast, her natural balance was discovered. The exact combination of canvas that caused her to labor the least as the wind shifted from point to point was studied and noted. No doubt many officers did all of this in a half-conscious way. Most of them probably responded to emergencies just as the experienced driver of a car does, automatically, doing the right thing in less time than it would take to decide what the right thing was.

In both cases, experience is what counts. But the theory lies behind the experience. The man with a true mental picture of the mechanics of his machine—car or sailing ship—can train himself to run it better, and to respond more accurately, even when he calls his response instinct. A car driver who does not understand the function of the spark plug and the firing cycle will "ride" the accelerator when his engine begins to knock toward the top of a hill. He hopes to get extra power by pushing harder on what seems to be the source of power. But the one who realizes what a knock means—that part of the power is opposing the rest—will ease up on the accelerator and nurse his car over the final part of the ascent by giving it no more fuel than it can properly use.

It was and is the same, in principle, with the sailing machine. Windage—that part of the wind blowing against hull, masts, and rigging—is like the knock of the engine. It is part of the general source of power, but it is working in opposition to the portion which is being twisted in a useful direction by the leverage of the sails.

An officer who had come to know his ship by studying its behavior constantly, under all sorts of circumstances, would have an automatic sense of what he could expect of her, especially in such crucial situations as that in which the brig *Betsey* found herself, off a crescent-shaped lee shore.

The main practical item which every officer had to discover was, "How close will she sail to the wind?" This factor, for the convenience of the steersman, was expressed in "points" of the compass card. The complete compass circle of 360° is divided into 32 points—North, North by East, North-Northeast, Northeast by North, Northeast, etc. If we divide the number of points into the total number of degrees in a circle we will get $11\frac{1}{4}°$ to each point. Lookouts, when they call "Light, three points off the port bow," mean that they see a light at an angle of something like $33\frac{3}{4}°$ to the left of a line straight ahead.

When it was said that a ship would sail within six points of the wind, the speaker meant that she would make positive forward progress against, say, a north wind, if the steersman kept her at an angle of six times $11\frac{1}{4}°$ or $67\frac{1}{2}°$ with the direction of the wind. In this position, with her yards hauled as nearly fore-and-aft as the disposition of the rigging would allow, she would get a little more than enough wind in her sails to overcome the contrary forces set up by the wind blowing against her topsides, masts, and rigging.

A fore-and-aft rigged vessel, such as a schooner—with less rigging, freeboard, and superstructure to set up opposing forces—could haul her booms more closely to the line of the keel, and might sail within three points of the wind. The contrary push created by the other exposed surfaces offered less opposition to cancel the power got from the sails. In the case of a square rigger there also was a practical limit to the extent to which her yards could usefully be hauled around. The luffs of the sails tended to tremble and take part of the wind on the wrong surface. The rigging which kept the masts steady got more and more in the way of the sails themselves, the more sharply the yards were braced.

The final calculation, in the case of the *Betsey* off the coral reef, lay between a pair of bad choices: to get more forward speed and less leeway by sailing within seven points of the wind, or to try to "claw off shore" as much as possible by sailing toward a point more comfortably wide of the end of the reef. In the latter case the leeway—or slip sidewise—would be greater and might lose in the long run more distance than would be gained by pointing nearer to the wind. There was never an exact answer to such a problem, because much would depend upon the set of the currents. But the officer who knew his ship and understood the principles of leverage behind her conduct would be in a better position to make a shrewder bet on that part of the problem which was always admittedly guesswork.

Hearing of such situations, any mechanically minded boy in Nat Palmer's world hardly could fail to day-dream on ways and means of making all vessels more weatherly. Boys of Stonington had the choice of turning their imaginations seaward, to such problems as these, or of looking inland to quieter years at dairy farming, the only other local industry of importance. Those who chose seafaring, as most did, could think about the *Betsey* and about Parson Avery's sermons stressing the providence of God in arousing Captain Fanning from sleep to warn him of danger.

Down in the shipyards, however, there were Unitarian carpenters whose religion gave them the different view that God's goodness was principally displayed in developing the skill of shipwrights, when he guided their hands in the moulding and fashioning of more weatherly vessels that would thus be made capable in advance of clawing off a lee shore when they discovered they were on one.

Next to the cannibal-befriended sailors who came swaggering home from the sea's ends, these shipwrights were the most admirable men in Nat Palmer's world. Small boys of Stonington grew up knee deep in the chips and sawdust of the Palmer yard. Clean chips the size of your hand, from adz or broad ax, cushioned the ground everywhere. The sawdust collected mainly in the bottom of a pit. The principal frame timbers of even a sloop were so large and heavy that the simplest means of sawing them to shape was to prop a rough log across the top of a trench in which one man whipped the lower end of a long saw while his partner, the top sawyer, stood on the timber itself—guiding the blade along the chalk mark.

Sawdust collected a foot deep in the bottom of the saw-pit before it was shoveled out. When there were no sawyers at work, the boys of Stonington found there an excellent mattress upon which to leap. A quick run and a jump from one end of the oblong pit might carry the jumper nearly twenty feet to the opposite end.

The shipwrights ought not to have minded. Seamen were needed to man the vessels shipwrights made. Such games helped to develop the courage and quickness expected of Stonington's younger citizens, many of whom signed articles as royal boys before they were in their 'teens. Their town was referred to all along the coast as the "cradle of seamen."

Stonington, from which Nat Palmer's world so quickly expanded, occupies a little finger of land that points down from the eastern end of Connecticut's shoreline as if to remind its mariners of the course past Montauk to the Antarctic seas. Stonington men, in the early Eighteen Hundreds, already were crisscrossing one another's sea tracks in the remotest waters of the world. But they were beginning to stake out as particularly their own the cold regions of the deep South Atlantic, the islands scattered off Argentina, Patagonia, and Chile. As Nat himself neared his 'teens, it was inevitable that he would turn his eyes in that direction too. But at the time when he might have been expected to seek service in a sealer, all such Antarctic enterprises were interrupted by a recurrence of the events of the Revolution. Joshua Humphreys had been right when he wrote that the United States "at a future day" might "be dragged into a war with . . . powers of the Old Continent, especially Great Britain." Antarctic voyages were postponed because of a greater need for American vessels in other services.

At least Humphreys' frigates were ready for the emergency. And a few more particulars about the exact ways in which Humphreys had foreseen their problems are now in order.

CHAPTER TEN

IN STORIES OF THE OLD SEA FIGHTS, THE TERM "WEATHER gage" frequently appears. The ship with the weather gage was nearer to the compass point from which the wind was blowing. As most ships sailed more and more slowly and were trickier to handle the "nearer" to the wind they were pointed, it was obviously an advantage to be nearer the wind to begin with.

The opponent, in trying to approach a ship that had the weather gage of him, would be able to use only a small fraction of the wind's power, because his yards would have to be braced up sharp. The ship with the weather gage could maintain more speed, to execute any maneuver more quickly. A sharp, single-decked ship lying low in the water could easily get the weather gage of a double-decker of the same length, and hold it. A double tier of guns called for topsides nearly twice as high above waterline as those of a single-decker. The wind blowing against the higher wooden sides of the larger ship would give it more leeway.

A ship capable of sailing at a rate of five miles an hour straight ahead, when hauled up as close to the wind as she could go, might be blown two miles sidewise in the process if she were a single-decker, and three miles if she were a double-decker. Sooner or later the lower, more "weatherly" ship would be "up wind" from the double-decker. The frigate could then lie over on the other tack and run toward her enemy at greater speed, with the wind behind her. She would now perhaps be making ten knots, and would be able to take up new positions with a rapidity greater than that of her bigger enemy. The frigate could choose the most advantageous angle from which to get in a broadside.

The larger naval guns, until the middle of the last century, were always mounted on wooden carriages and could be moved only a little way to left or right. A broadside had to be fired straight outward from the gun ports. As is now the case with single-place fighter aircraft, the guns were aimed by aiming the whole ship. The pursuit ship of today aims head-on, but the old fighting ship had to swing broadside-on to aim her heavy guns. That was the main reason why the ship with the weather gage had so great an advantage. It was in a position to swoop down speedily upon the other. If the enemy turned tail to the wind to get up speed, the pursuer could swing suddenly across the stern of his prey and let go a broadside.

The old sailing men-of-war seldom had more than one or

two guns that could be fired straight ahead or astern. Therefore the trick was to sail your ship toward the enemy in such a way that you would keep out of the line of fire of his broadside guns until you could pour a broadside into his bow or stern, from which he could not reply effectively. This was called "raking." It meant that well-aimed shot would travel the whole length of the deck, perhaps 150 feet, instead of the 45 feet or so across the beam. Raking fire gave the shot three or four times as great a chance of doing damage.

From this it can be seen that a smaller ship, if it could get the weather gage of a bigger and clumsier one, could dart down to place its shots in the most vulnerable position, and be well away again before the enemy could get his broadside swung around to aim. But the ability to do so of course depended largely upon "blowing weather," as Humphreys foresaw. In a calm or in light winds the bigger ship would have ample time to be towed or sailed into position to hurl broadsides into the smaller ones as it approached.

The other factor Humphreys had in mind was the difficulty of using the lower tier of guns in a double-decker at all. When the waves were high the lower gunports on the leeward side of the larger ship, and perhaps on both sides, had to be kept closed. This had the effect of turning a 64-gun ship into a frigate anyhow, by putting about 14 guns out of action on each side. Moreover, the covering of the lower gunports was comparatively thin, and provided vulnerable spots to shoot at near the waterline. A frigate then could attack such a handicapped enemy even from the leeward, on equal terms, broadside for broadside: but the frigate could do so only if she was armed with the same caliber guns as those carried by a double-decker. And this, before Humphreys' frigates put to sea, was never the case.

That brings us to Humphreys' final specifications. With the doubtful aid of another Quaker ship designer named Fox, Humphreys prepared drafts of his fighting ships. All were to be 10 or 15 feet longer than the standard frigates of Europe. Their principal timbers were to be as heavy as those of a double-decked fighting ship. This would render them able to carry long 24-pounders where other frigates carried 18-pounders, with 32-pounder carronades on the quarter-deck where frigates ordinarily carried 24's. With these provisions attended to, their lines under water were to be as well formed as possible for the purpose of getting to windward.

So it was that Joshua Humphreys, nearly twenty years ahead of time, foresaw clearly what the United States would be up against in a war with a first-rate naval power. Secretary of War Knox, acting temporarily as Secretary of the Navy, corresponded with a number of shipwrights before he convinced himself that Humphreys was his man. And Humphreys, designing his frigates on the basis of knowledge accumulated under the blockades, made the first decisive advance toward the ultimate refinement of entirely American design that was to appear fifty years later in the Yankee clipper fleet.

But the basic principle he revealed to Robert Morris in 1793, and put into the solid form on the stocks in 1797, had been impressed upon the designer as early as 1778, because of the fate of his first naval vessel, the *Randolph*.

Three things, most clearly, had been wrong with her. She had not been fast enough to run from a bigger enemy. She had not been big enough to contend with even an average member of her own frigate class. Her topsides had been too thinly constructed to stop the red-hot shot that got through and dropped into her powder magazine.

The chief things to remember about Humphreys' frigates are these: They were not a wonderful new design, better because of their mould than existing ships of the same size. They were a new class, midway in size between the larger foreign frigates and the smaller fourth rates. They were a little wider on deck than standard frigates, and so were able to carry guns individually as large as those in ships of the line. Their topsides were as strong as those of fourth rates, their frames as heavy as those of third rates. The loss in speed that might have resulted from this extra solidity of construction was balanced off by some refinement of their lines under water—but they were not, as some writers have claimed, sharp enough to be called forerunners of the clipper mould. Nevertheless, by a very shrewd balance of strength and weight, of mould and sail plan, they proved as a group to be faster than any other class of fighting ships then in existence, whether larger or smaller.

The chief virtue of the Humphreys design was a willingness to forget precedent. It was accompanied by a belief that fewer and better individual ships were the only possible effective answer to nations that already had a tremendous head start.

This principle, established dramatically in the first fleet of the official United States Navy, carried over into commercial shipbuilding. The packet trade of the Atlantic was almost completely captured from foreign countries in the Eighteen Twenties and Eighteen Thirties because Yankee shipowners had the foresight to build better and faster packets, gambling a sacrifice of cargo capacity against the chance of making enough extra trips to compensate.

It was the same willingness to try the new idea that made the Yankee packet lines establish regular sailing dates which passengers and shippers of freight could count on, no matter what the weather was like. The Yankee packets sailed on the dot, even if the hold and the cabins were largely empty. This unheard-of behavior paid in the long run.

It paid so well that when financial conditions, in the Eighteen Forties, made the clippers possible, both owners and builders were accustomed to the Humphreys idea that the best way to cope with an adversary is not by the weight of numbers but by new ideas and the excellence of single achievements.

In that sense Joshua Humphreys, if not the father, was surely the grandfather of the clipper-ship era.

CHAPTER ELEVEN

Nathaniel brown palmer was born august 8th, 1799, midway between two naval wars. His home town of Stonington found its first bombardment hard to forget. But even as the memory dwindled, evidences grew stronger that the days of blockade would come again. Warfare flickered all around the edges of the Atlantic, at the turn of the century, and might have spread from any of a dozen points.

On the very morning of young Nat's birth, Secretary of the Navy Stoddert sent orders to Captain Campbell to make the best of his way, in the United States brig-of-war *Eagle*, to Guadeloupe Station in the West Indies. There Campbell was to co-operate with Captain Tingey of the *Ganges* "for the protection of our Commerce & the punishment of the French Vessels & people who depredate upon it." France and the United States had not gone through the formalities of declaring war against each other, but their ships were engaged in naval battles none the less.

A few years later, the growing strength of Napoleon so strained the resources of the British navy that its captains became desperate for men, and took them by force in increasing numbers from American ships. The bitter wrangle over impressment grew out of a difference in the laws of the two countries. England contended that a man who once had been an Englishman was always an Englishman. But the United States was largely peopled by men who had once been Englishmen.

It seems to have been the general English policy not to molest anyone actually born in the area that had become the United States, but to seize all naturalized Americans who had been born in England. This always left room for an argument. American seamen carried "protections" in the form of documents proving their American birth. English officers, examining these documents, had a strange habit of mislaying them, or of tearing them up with the blunt statement that they were obvious forgeries.

In such cases, the man with the bigger guns was likely to do what he thought he had to do, for the sake of his own ship's efficiency. To be undermanned was to risk disaster in a fight. The long series of wars had drained England of seamen. Each English captain was responsible for the recruiting of his own men. With Napoleon preparing to invade England itself, and succeeding everywhere on the continent of Europe, it was perhaps too much to expect of a patriotic British captain that he be entirely scrupulous.

Some honest mistakes were made, and more dishonest ones. Many British captains did not bother even to make excuses. They took the men they needed and gave necessity as the reason. So it appears, at least, from the reports of American merchant skippers to their owners and to the Navy Department. Stonington parents, like those in every other Atlantic seaport, had their share of sons impressed into service in the British navy.

Even so, when Jefferson's government in 1807 forbade all American ships to trade with the warring powers of Europe, hoping thereby to enforce respect for American rights, Nat Palmer's neighbors bitterly objected. Shipowners of Connecticut preferred the risks of trade in wartime to the poverty which came from no foreign trade at all. Congress, perceiving that the measure was harming America more than it was helping her, permitted limited trade again in 1809—when Nat Palmer was ten years old— but conditions drifted from difficult to exasperating, and many believed war inevitable long before it finally came, in 1812.

British agents were aware of the sentiment in our New England states, including Connecticut. They reported that the northern hotheads who had plunged into revolution without waiting for the other colonies to make up their minds were not so enthusiastic about this second looming war. Therefore, to keep from antagonizing the political party that refused to support the government in Washington, the British restricted their second blockade in 1812 to more southerly waters, off Delaware and Chesapeake Bays.

Purposely, for many months, they left the coasting trade of New England and Long Island Sound unmolested, and even provided deliberate safe-conduct for New England ships bound to Europe with supplies for the allies of England in her fight against Napoleon. The feeling against the Federal policy was so bitter in Boston that when Bainbridge arrived at that port in *Old Ironsides,* after his victory over His Majesty's frigate *Java,* the officials of the city treated him almost as if he were the enemy. It was the common people who took him to their hearts, and it was the pressure of the common people that gradually brought New England into reluctant support of the interests of the nation as a whole.

Residents of Nat Palmer's town got their first visual evidence of serious fighting when Humphreys' frigate *United States,* Commodore Decatur, sailed past Fisher's Island on December 4th, 1812, to anchor at the mouth of the Thames, off New London. News came that she had sent her prize, the British frigate *Macedonian,* into Newport. The *Macedonian* had been so damaged by American gunfire, in an action south of the Azores, that bad weather off Block Island had made it seem advisable to her prize crew to run for a port easier to reach than New London.

Stonington then realized that war was on in earnest, and that there would be reprisals. The town was divided in its own mind between pride in the first major naval victory of the war, and misgivings about the wisdom of being at war at all. While Napoleon's France still remained as Old England's major enemy, New Englanders had a strong hankering not to aid the new brand of tyrant by warring against their British cousins at the same time.

But the sea fight between the frigates *United States* and *Macedonian* proved too big a spark to be suppressed.

Stupid cruelties inflicted by British landing parties in the central Atlantic states fanned national indignation until the conflict spread north and south along our coasts and seaward even into the Pacific.

The first major single ship action went far to prove how right Humphreys had been in setting forth the principles upon which to commence building a United States navy—principles that culminated in the clipper ships. It also was a signal for the extension of Britain's blockade.

On March 30th, 1813, by Order in Council, the policy already effective off the Delaware capes was extended northward to New York, closing one exit used by Connecticut shipping. The British Commodore Warren still strove to exempt most of New England from the effects of the blockade, hoping to keep opinion divided within the United States. But in the long run it proved impossible. On November 16th, 1813, Long Island Sound inside Montauk and Black Points was included, by his proclamation, in the blockaded area. Technically this left Stonington still free. That was scant comfort, as it bottled up practically all of the trade passing to and fro upon which Stonington depended.

So matters stood when young Nat Palmer, aged fourteen, first signed articles as a professional mariner. Having divided most of his hours out of school between the shipyards and the fishing boats of Stonington, he had little to learn about the principles of sailing vessels as they then were understood. But he plunged into one of the periods when skill and daring were most needed, because the vessel he chose was a blockade-runner. She was on a regular run, carrying supplies between New York and the eastern part

of the state of Massachusetts, then known as the district of
Maine.

This time Long Island remained in American hands, but
the narrow channels leading out of New York's Lower Bay
could be corked up with such ease by the British blockaders
that coasters from the north preferred the Sound route in
their efforts to deliver goods at the metropolis. The passage
between Stonington and Montauk, fifteen miles or so wide,
offered better chances of slipping past the enemy. Its shoals
and reefs, among which dangerous tide rips developed,
were at times more of a help than a hindrance. They could
be skirted more closely by a little coaster than by a sizable
pursuing man-of-war.

Such a boy as Nat Palmer, who had sailed those waters
from infancy, could use the lead line to tell where he was,
even in the dark or in a fog, by noting the combined evidences of depth and character of bottom. Under usual conditions a seaman would climb down in to the fore chains,
swing the lead a few times to give it momentum, then
whirl it in a complete circle—up forward, back overhead,
down with a rush—releasing it as it swept forward and began to rise again. The idea was to heave the lead far enough
forward to give it time to settle just as the heaver himself
came over the point at which it touched bottom. Then,
feeling the line perpendicular and tense, with the lead
barely touching, he would note the depth with the aid of
"marks" and "deeps" arranged in a fashion similar to that
of the markers of the log line.

Black strips of leather were tied in to mark 2 and 3
fathoms, or 12 and 18 feet respectively above the bottom
surface of the lead. A white bunting marker came at 5

fathoms, a red one at 7, black leather again at 10, white bunting at 13 and 15, red bunting at 17, followed by less frequent markers for greater depths. The lead itself was pear-shaped, flat-bottomed, with a cup hollowed in the

lower surface. Into the cup a little fresh tallow was pressed, to bring up evidence of what the bottom was like.

Most of the shoals had their distinguising features. Some were pure white sand, some mixed white and black, some speckled with broken shell. By observing such features of the evidence, brought up sticking to the tallow, the experienced coastwise sailor could tell about where he was, even in the darkness. If he combined this evidence with observations of the rate at which the depth increased or decreased, he was often able to say over which side of a particular shoal he was passing, and so determine his location with an error of not more than a few hundred feet.

During the blockade, it was advisable to drift along without a sound. Then the lead would be carried forward by a second seaman who would lower it gently from the bowsprit to avoid the splash and plumping sound that came with a regular heave. After the depth had been noted by the man in the fore chains, he would pass the lead in-board to be inspected under cover of the bulwarks, by the light of a shielded bull's-eye lantern, for evidence of the kind of bottom. Such efforts to creep through the darkness or fog, past the blockaders, using an accurate knowledge of the offshore grounds, provided one of the two principal chances of avoiding capture. The other way was to run for it—to exercise speed and skillful management of a complicated sailing machine bristling with controls.

The controlling wheels and levers of today's machines, with their dozens of corresponding gauges and meter needles (as on the instrument board of a night bomber) are not very different in basic principle from the equally numerous controls on a sailing vessel. Reading the altimeter is easier than the corresponding process of heaving the lead, but both serve the same essential purpose. Rudder and compass are still much the same as ever, on both flying and sailing machines. The modern calculations of drift, like the older calculations of leeway, are but good guesses at best.

As an airplane pilot now keeps his gaze wandering over the surfaces of many instruments, making the occasional adjustments demanded for peak performance, so the officers of a sailing vessel watched shrewdly the tension of scores of separate ropes, the trim of many spars. These indicators served the same purposes as the needles on our modern dials but they called for more individual judgment. The officer would order a short haul now and then, here or there, to maintain his own sensitive, wooden-and-hemp machine at maximum efficiency.

Sometimes, amid all our glittering newness, we lose sight of the fact that all the tools and machines we use are only extensions of our own muscles. They still must answer, just as our arms and legs answer, to a human intelligence. The robot pilot can land a great bomber if the airfield is ready to receive it. But the same kind of intelligence was built into the best sailing ships. The pilot says, of a well-designed and rightly loaded plane, that she "flies herself." In sailing ship days, it similarly was said that a ship sailed herself. With her controls properly adjusted, the sails efficiently set and the wheel lashed, a well-designed and rightly laded sailing ship would come back to her course when she fell away.

Not long ago a big airplane, deserted by her crew in mid-air near Florida, flew to Mexico before she crashed. Sailing ships too have gone great distances of their own accord, after they had been deserted as unsafe. But these voyages are aimless. Human brains, human hands and feet, make contact with the mechanism and give it a purpose.

The problem of evading the blockaders off the mouth of Long Island Sound was little different in its essentials from that of getting past a screen of fighters, and through a barrage of flak, on the way to a bombing objective. When each side has similar equipment, courage and ingenuity become the deciding factors, whether the equipment is made from aluminum alloys and from plastics, or from wood and the fibers of hemp and cotton.

The real story, in any age, is to be found in the use and improvement of the equipment at hand.

Blockaders changed the use, and forced the improvement, of sailing machines in Nat Palmer's world.

CHAPTER TWELVE

Let us get back into the problem personally, as if we were at sea again in the fifty-ton sloop *Fortune*, Dennis master, out of Portland, bound for New York. A fresh breeze does not altogether flatten the musty, dry tang of salted codfish, or the reek of whale oil taken on at Nantucket, which make up the bulk of our cargo. You and I can begin to see each other in the dawn: passengers of innocent appearance. But I have a score of large bills of exchange sewn into the skirts of my blue broadcloth coat, and you have dispatches concealed in your green one.

A knife ripped down the right seam will get the papers out for destruction, if it should come to that.

We lean forward with the polite curiosity of the amateur

as Captain Dennis takes the dripping lead and turns his bull's-eye lantern upon it under the gunwale.

"Shell and coarse brown sand."

"No shell in the last cast, sir?"

"No shell, boy. We should be coming up with Weeka-paug."

"Yes, sir, about three mile offshore, when it's at five fathoms."

Young Nat Palmer straightens for a look shoreward, and then around the forward horizon, slowly. He pauses, looks hard.

"Sail, sir, to larboard and abeam."

After peering closely for a minute or two, the rest of us catch the faint glimmer. The captain holds his course.

A little later young Nat says softly, "The *Eolus*, sir," and then, "She's seen us."

The boy looks inquiringly at the skipper. You and I, conscious of our valuable coattails, wonder what we would do. The captain is judging his distances. Noyes Point at Weekapaug is three miles almost directly to starboard. The frigate *Eolus* of the blockading squadron has begun to wear about, midway in her reach to sea. Obviously she has seen us or she would be casting upon the other tack instead.

We cannot run straight away from her. The wind is blowing from her to us, directly inshore. She has the weather gage. There is no shelter for us short of Watch Hill Point, seven or eight miles to the westward. Stonington Harbor, the first possibly safe anchorage, is four miles beyond that. A shallow shoreline of continuous sand and rocks invites at best an attempt to scuttle the sloop, or a quick run aground and a wallowing ashore of all hands before the frigate's boats arrive to try to tow her off as a prize.

Even as amateurs, we have an inkling of Captain Dennis's problem. The frigate, up wind, can close in at her pleasure, sailing at her best speed with the wind on her quarter. We must decide whether it is best at first to sail offshore, tacking slightly against the wind at a rate slower than the frigate's. This would get us the advantage of wind abeam a little later when we must make the last dash for safety around Watch Hill Point.

There is a natural, panicky desire to keep as far from the enemy as possible, all the way, hugging the curving shoreline. But that would bring the wind ahead of us as we neared the outthrust point and tried to get around it. We should then be going at our slowest when we might have the most need of speed. Moreover, we should be traveling a curving course along the cupped shoreline while the frigate could move straight for our common destination and thus have the better chance of cutting us out.

Captain Dennis holds to his former course until the intentions of the frigate are unmistakable. Then, with a word or two to the steersman, he reveals to us his decision that the boldest course is the best. The little *Fortune* comes up into the wind, standing out to sea across the bows of her pursuer. The distance narrows to a mile, a half-mile.

There is a puff of smoke from the frigate's bow chaser. The round shot kicks up a little jet of spume midway between us. The *Fortune* is very weatherly, as small vessels go. Yet it takes her nearly half an hour to make a mile of actual progress, and in this time the frigate—on a more favorable wind—has sailed three times as far.

The round shot was intended more as a signal than as

an effort to reach us. But at the present rates it is only a matter of minutes before we shall be in range.

Captain Dennis stands to the tiller himself, allowing her to pay off a little. The sloop no longer pitches against the choppy waves, as she sails large, gathering speed. The frigate's officer of the deck has observed the change in her motion and progress. One of his bow chasers speaks again. The ball, fired for maximum range, falls with a small splash a hundred yards off our port quarter.

It is as close as Captain Dennis wants them to come. He puts the tiller up and with a flowing sheet sets a straight course for Watch Hill Point. The *Eolus* gains less obviously now. When we are still a mile from the point she tries again with a bow chaser. The ball falls wide a few yards, and perhaps fifty astern. The next one all but reaches us, but Captain Dennis has calculated well. He is racing for the shoal water inside Gangway Rock. The frigate is too close inshore already. She alters her course for the next entrance, between Watch Hill Reef and Sugar Reef. She must sail a triangle while we can run straight for the last obstruction between us and our harbor.

Twenty minutes later, as we come up with Napatree Point, her round shot again are close, but she is again forced off by the shoal across which we are able to set a straight course for the safe anchorage of Stonington, now less than two miles away.

Nat Palmer had many experiences of the same general sort, during the years of the blockade. They could hardly have left any doubts in his mind that the best uses to which a young man could turn his ingenuity lay in the improvement of the speed and weatherliness of sailing vessels.

There was an opposite side to the medal. More and more, as the Old World fought for colonial territories in the latter Seventeen and the early Eighteen Hundreds, trading vessels were organized into convoys. It has happened again, for similar reasons, in our times. Old records frequently refer to a fleet of a hundred sail or more, protected by several frigates and third or fourth rates. When merchant ships were herded together, speed might be a positive peril. In stormy weather a fast vessel might not be able to keep from outrunning its convoy in the darkness. There was little incentive in that period to increase the speed of the average merchant ship belonging to any country that had adopted the convoy system. But the United States had far too few men-of-war to organize an effective convoy system. Our ordinary merchantman was designed to fend for itself.

A maritime state of affairs which tended to encourage Americans to improve the speed of merchant shipping thus at the same time was operating to make Englishmen and Frenchmen content with average droghers which would stow more cargo, more profitably, at average convoy speed. Enormous efforts were made in 1942 and 1943 to expand our merchant fleet, in the belief that it was better to build a hundred ordinary standardized ships and lose a third of them in one voyage in convoy than to build fewer and faster ones in the expectation that they might get a larger proportion of the total cargo to port. It may have been the wiser course, under particular conditions, but we need to remember that it is the one which stifles initiative and competition in design.

Yet speed is not always the most important factor in

ship design. When two vessels have the same carrying capacity, and have cost the same amount to build, the one that develops more speed from equal power is obviously the more efficient of the two. But in some trades, and for some uses, the extra ingenuity which produced the speedier vessel might better have been spent in providing larger cargo capacity.

The perfect machine, at any time and for any particular use, is the one that performs with the greatest efficiency, and speed is not in all cases efficient.

If an average chunky vessel, on an average slow convoy passage of seven weeks from the West Indies to England, could carry 500 tons of cargo safely, there would have been no point in using a faster vessel of the same value that could carry only 300 tons, unless that vessel could get along without convoy protection and make about two voyages while the other was making only one. The faster carrier would have had to be so very much faster than usual that it could feel confident of outrunning the enemy's cruisers and privateers.

For the merchant marine, the test of a successful design was, and still remains, the record of consistent net earnings. Speed became important to shipowners only when it began to mean greater profits, not per voyage, but per year. An extremely fast ship might have been a good investment for an Englishman in convoy days, but a moderately fast one was not. In general, then, the tendency was to build the most capacious vessel possible that could make average convoy speed.

While the War of 1812 was being fought, most British trade used the convoy system, and most American merchantmen fended for themselves. Privateers of both countries were very numerous. The record of their captures and recaptures was approximately even. American privateers hovered on the flanks of the great convoys, ready to dart in and cut out the stragglers. British privateers roamed the waters seaward from their own blockading squadrons, to pester the individual Yankees who stood off and on, waiting for favorable weather to run the blockade.

But of all these wartime influences that made the shipowners of the United States value speed as the first virtue in a sailing vessel, the record of Humphreys' frigates was the most dramatic and impressive. It was brought home by the first major action of the war at sea. Captain Decatur's frigate, the *United States*, was 176 feet long on deck. Her prize, the frigate *Macedonian*, was 10 feet shorter. Both vessels carried 30 guns on the main deck at the time of the action, but those of the *United States* fired 24-pound shot, while the *Macedonian's* were 18-pounders. The Americans won, primarily, because they had a better, bigger, more heavily armed ship, and they felt a bit embarrassed about it. One of the victorious officers wrote, not long after the triumph, "I am well aware it will be said, the *Macedonian* is a little ship, with five guns less than the *United States*, and a hundred men less, and carries lighter metal &c. Well, this is true—she is inferior in all these, but she is just such a ship as the English have achieved all their single ship victories in . . . and have till the *Guerrière's* loss, always thought a match for any single decked ship afloat."

Our school histories which overlook such facts, not only underrate the skill of brave Englishmen who faced superior odds, but tend also to obscure the major reason why the United States was not completely defeated.

The real triumph of the American navy is not to be looked for in the individual successes of our bigger frigates, which consistently defeated the smaller English ones. That, by a naval tactitian, was to be taken for granted. The triumphant fact is that the navy of the United States could make any impression at all upon the most powerful fleet in the world. England had about a thousand warships in 1812. The United States possessed exactly two dozen. The three best of these were rated at 44 guns apiece, as compared with the British maximum of over 100 guns per ship.

During the War of 1812, the Connecticut region except Stonington itself was not treated as harshly by the enemy as it had been in the Revolution. Admiral Sir Thomas Hardy, who enforced the blockade, even paid fair prices for the food and stores he seized from civilians. But Yankee ingenuity finally angered that amiable Briton, when home-made torpedoes, and booby traps aboard captured small craft, began to explode around his vessels. Stonington was suspected as the place of manufacture of these deadly contraptions, which had cost the lives of several British seamen.

On August 9th, 1814, the admiral consequently stood in, gave notice of one hour to civilians, and then let go with the guns of his squadron: a ship-of-the-line, a frigate, and two brigs.

Nat Palmer's town proved hard to punish. It mounted in its defensive battery only two 18-pounders and one 4-pounder, but the more than fifteen tons of projectiles thrown ashore by the squadron's 160 guns inflicted only one serious wound among the defenders, who with their

three small cannon caused 71 casualties in one enemy vessel alone—the only one of which records survive. The attacks, continuing throughout four days, were all repelled.
Stonington youngsters for years afterwards enjoyed chant-
ing,

> *"It cost the king ten thousand pounds*
> *To have a go at Stonington."*

Unless luck brought him home for his fifteenth birthday,
the day before the bombardment, foremasthand Nat Palmer seems not to have been in the vicinity. At least the
surviving Palmer papers nowhere mention it. But the fight
put up by Stonington against fifty-to-one ordnance odds
shows us the prevailing attitude of the people among whom
Nat Palmer grew up, in the cradle of seamen. Sensible mili-
tary men, faced by such odds, would immediately have
evacuated the town. That possibility seems never to have
occurred to Nat Palmer's neighbors.

American school books sometimes mention that unimportant skirmish. But they hasten past the most important
point of all, in connection with our War of 1812. This is
that England had Napoleon to deal with at the same time.
Early in the American conflict, England could spare but
few of her warships from the coasts of Europe and the
essential convoys. After the first Peace of Paris, the English
might have been expected to turn their major naval squadrons westward: a crushing force against which even the
five best frigates in the world would have been of little use.

But everyone was sick of the seemingly endless fighting
in Europe. Napoleon at first was sent only as far as Elba.
The tyrant's first downfall left the politics of a whole con-

tinent still in need of close watching. Many nations had to be established anew. The British fleet held its stations around the European coasts.

England's statesmen claimed that she had fought the Napoleonic wars chiefly to free the world of a tyrant. Even if that was not the real reason, it would have been bad politics for the British to begin to behave tyrannically, at such a moment, towards their former American possessions. A treaty of peace was drawn up in 1814. At that time the only considerable American victory on land had not yet been fought. News of the peace arrived at New Orleans only after the battle was over. Thus the American commissioners, who were able to put through an agreement which really called the war a draw, had no land successes to use as bargaining points. The American fleets had triumphed on the Great Lakes, but the American invasion of Canada had failed disastrously. The British held our own national capital. Their close blockade of our coasts was unbroken.

The only strength our commissioners had behind their efforts was the impression made upon the whole world by the brilliant successes of Humphreys' few frigates. That record, and the still uncertain internal fate of Europe, made it possible for them to call the war off by a common-sense agreement, mainly because the people in both countries were tired of paying for it in heavy taxes and ruined trade.

It was a good thing for both sides, because Napoleon broke loose again in the spring of 1815 for the Hundred Days that were brought to a close only after the Battle of Waterloo.

Neither the British nor the Americans succeeded in getting what they said they had been fighting for. But it was a near enough thing to disaster, for the United States, to bring national pride into play. Americans seized upon the memory of the successful single-ship actions in which their frigates had been victorious, and steadily remembered them while they forgot the humiliations of the burning of Washington and the defeats of the Canadian border. Collections of accounts of the sea fights tumbled by the thousands from the presses, bearing such titles as *The Naval Monument,* and *The Naval Temple.*

Glorying in those successes, partly to help forget other defeats, America fell in love with the idea of speed and good seamanship. Luck was with her. During the next four or five decades of general peace these factors became the most important ones of all. But good seamanship and speed do not always go hand in hand. This is demonstrated by the most dramatic event in the life of N. B. Palmer, one of the men who did most to make speed important in itself.

CHAPTER THIRTEEN

THERE IS AN OLD ARGUMENT IN THE MERCHANT SERVICE, as to whether the best captains "climbed up through the hawse hole or blew in at the cabin window," which was one way of admitting that many good commanders started as common seamen, and that many others were first appointed as officers on a basis of schooling rather than rough-and-tumble experience. Great examples of both sorts have occurred, of course, or there would have been no argument.

Nat Palmer squeezed through the hawse hole. After his breathless, early experiences in a blockade runner had ended with the Treaty of Ghent, he continued in the coasting trade, winning command of the schooner *Galena* before he was out of his 'teens.

While he was employed near his home, other Stonington seamen were beginning to make a specialty of hunting seals on the islands lying off South America. Stonington's Captain Edmund Fanning was one of the first to profit in this trade. So many others followed that the herds of seals were nearly exterminated in twenty years of stupid butchery. Midway in the period, sealskin prices fell to a tenth of what they had been, because the market was glutted. Then the scarcity of live seals raised prices again. Stonington men began to run along the watery tracks of old rumors, seeking islands that might or might not exist, hoping to find new herds of seals.

In Nat Palmer's younger days, Cape Horn was not yet the bogey it later became. Stonington men seem to have taken the bitter hardships of "Old Cape Stiff" quite as a matter of course. They sailed by preference to and fro in the very waters the clipper-ship men later did their utmost to be through and away from as speedily as possible.

It was into such cold, foggy, stormy wastes of desolation that the seals could be presumed to have retreated from their relentless hunters. If they were to be found at all, the best chance of finding them lay in seeking the worst, ice-armored outposts of the world.

Such were the "Lost Auroras," islands of hearsay that supposedly had been seen by two or three gale-swept mariners who were sailing by dead reckoning at the time, and who when next they got trustworthy observations of their latitude had been blown too far to find their uncertain discoveries again. Some said they were only "ice islands," as icebergs then were usually called by the New Englanders. Others believed in them as vast seal rookeries. It was even romantically contended that they were rich in gold and precious stones.

The depressed state of the sealing industry, between 1815 and 1820, made a real search for the Auroras seem worth the gamble. Captain Edmund Fanning, who twenty years earlier had brought the *Betsey* home from the first round-the-world voyage out of the port of New York, was one of the principal merchants who interested themselves in the exploring venture. The brig *Hersilia*, newly completed at Stonington, was chosen for the voyage. She was 68 feet in length, 22 feet in beam. Obviously she had not been built to serve as a blockade runner. Her ratio of length to breadth was only 3.1 to 1. In Captain Fanning's own account of his voyages and enterprises, however, he mentions that she was coppered and excellently fitted out. It is probable that her builders had had such a voyage in view, and had designed her to be "burthensome"—capable of carrying a large cargo—as well as strong.

In the sealing trade, as in whaling, speed was relatively unimportant. The vessel would be anchored for months anyhow, while the cargo was being gathered. She probably would encounter floating ice. Terrific Antarctic storms could be expected as a matter of course. Sailing largely in uncharted seas, she might strike upon unknown reefs without warning. Speed at such a moment was the worst of faults.

With these considerations in mind, the *Hersilia* seems to have been an excellent vessel for her intended voyage. She was registered at the New London customs house by a brother of Edmund Fanning, and was put in command of James P. Sheffield. The brig and the voyage appealed so much to Nat Palmer, who was not quite twenty years of age, that he demoted himself from captain of a coaster to become second mate of the *Hersilia*. The owners, in checking up on Palmer's record, would have taken into account his blockade-running experiences. A knack for handling a vessel amongst reefs and shoals would obviously be useful in exploring the fabulous islands, if they displayed anything like the dangerous coasts upon which seal rookeries commonly were found.

The *Hersilia*, of 88 tons burden, sailed from Stonington on July 20th, 1819. Salt for the curing of skins probably was got aboard at Sal Island in the Cape Verde group, where it could be had for the shoveling from great dry deposits. Captain Sheffield procured most of his meat supply the cheapest way. He steered for the Falklands and there put his young second mate ashore with a seaman or two to kill the wild bullocks with which the islands had become stocked.

To make the best use of his time while Palmer was securing meat, Sheffield proceeded at once on his search for the Auroras. Some days later, Nat Palmer saw the sails of a brig in the offing. As she came closer to the coast where he was standing, he realized that she was not the *Hersilia* returning. When she had anchored, he discovered that she was a rival sealer.

Competition had become so keen and profits so scanty that no sealer was inclined to divulge his plans to another. But the master of the newcomer, the *Espirito Santo*, made some mystifying remarks about a new sealing ground for which he was about to sail. Although Nat helped him to get the meat he needed, even this service could not break the determined secrecy of the English captain of the brig with the Spanish name. He had been gone three days when Sheffield returned with the usual report—that the Auroras were still mythical. The second mate of the *Hersilia* then revealed that the English skipper might know where the Auroras were.

Young Nat had kept an eye on the *Espirito Santo*. Her captain, to keep his secret, had sailed a deceptive course at first. But he may not have reckoned with the fact that he was being watched by a youth who was destined soon to acquire a reputation for having the keenest eyesight of anyone afloat. The course of the *Espirito Santo* had been altered in time for Young Nat to have an excellent idea of the general direction in which she was bound.

The *Hersilia* had been looking for the Auroras south and west of the Horn. The fact that the *Espirito Santo* had sailed east of south convinced Captain Sheffield that it might be worth while to try to follow her, even though such accounts as there were of the Auroras all placed them in a different direction. Nat Palmer's observations of the other sealer's course accordingly were made the basis of the *Hersilia's* sailing directions. After four days, land was sighted in a position where none existed on the charts.

The land, upon closer inspection, broke up its contours into a series of dark, rugged islands, slashed here and there with gorges full of ice and snow. In a harbor of one of the islands the *Espirito Santo* lay at anchor. Her skipper regarded with good humor the success of Nat Palmer in tracking him to the South Shetlands, which had been definitely discovered only a year before by an Englishman who had kept his secret in order to allow English sealers to monopolize them. They may have been first seen more than a century earlier by the Dutch captain Gherritz, who reported land somewhere in the region. But Gherritz's observations were much too vague to prove it. It was upon his story indeed that the legends of the lost Auroras were largely based.

The English are reported in one account to have aided the Americans in securing a cargo of sealskins, in return for Nat Palmer's kindness when he helped them to get bullocks. These first two vessels to visit the new-found islands took an abundance of seals, and there was no immediate cause for rivalry. The *Hersilia* brought 10,000 skins back to Stonington. There, in accordance with the usual custom, both she and her cargo were sold in order that those who had invested in shares in the venture might settle their accounts at once and divide the profits.

Although the chief reasons for sharing risks had ended with the Napoleonic wars, this custom of selling ship and all after each voyage continued for many years until wealthy companies, or single individuals, began to regard themselves as the permanent owners of fleets of vessels large enough to balance up the risks. The development of marine insurance also helped to bring about the day when vessels were continuously retained in the service of one owner or company. Even then, the practice of selling most cargoes at auction as soon after their arrival as possible continued for many decades, until the expansion of the great shipping lines made it the usual thing for ships to carry other people's property almost entirely, at a fixed price per hundredweight or ton.

The earlier habit of selling ship as well as cargo after

each voyage can be considered as one of the many factors affecting the development of the clippers. Standard, reliable models of modest size and average condition brought steady, predictable returns. It became easier to improve ships, and to try new ideas, after shipowners as a rule began to consider them as permanent property. And that, in turn, became possible only when safety at sea and financial well-being made it no longer so necessary for several individuals to club together to invest their money in "a voyage."

This development was not due to take place until a decade or two after the return of the *Hersilia* from the South Shetlands. When she and her cargo were sold at public auction, everyone knew that a new sealing ground had been discovered. A number of expeditions soon were planned for the next season. As usual, when there is no governmental licensing to control wasteful attacks on natural resources, there was a prospect that the new herds would be speedily exterminated.

Even if Captain Sheffield had tried to keep the location of the South Shetlands a secret, in co-operation with the British, his own seamen could not all have been silenced. Other expeditions would have sought the services of some of them, to act as guides. In foreign ships, the common seaman was not encouraged to know anything about navigation, but in a rapidly expanding merchant marine such as America enjoyed at the time practically every boy before the mast had a good chance of becoming an officer in a few years, and studied accordingly.

The crew of the *Espirito Santo* might have been kept in ignorance of where they had been. But it would have been useless to try to keep such knowledge from the crew of the

Hersilia. The idea does not seem even to have occurred to the officers and owners. Our democracy was still in its extravagant youth. The "general welfare" phrase in the Constitution's preamble as yet seemed much less important than the "blessings of liberty" one immediately following it. Every man's right to rush and slaughter seals was unquestioned, even though the resulting crop of skins might well be so large as to drive prices down to a point where everyone would lose money, even though the unregulated butchery might exterminate the seals and end the business for all.

The answer of Stonington to this threat was typical under the circumstances, and for the times. The Stonington men decided to get there first, with a bigger fleet than anyone else. Where they had sent one vessel in 1819, they prepared to send eight in 1820. To keep track of the herds, and to discover new ones for so large a fleet to deal with, they selected one vessel especially as explorer, and to act as a tender to the others. For such duties she had to be small, to creep up near to dangerous coasts which the larger brigs could not approach. She had to provide some stowage space, to ferry off the skins from the camps. She had to be capable of sailing from Stonington to the Antarctic by herself, through all the weather that might be encountered in such a journey. She had to be commanded by a man thoroughly competent at such a variety of difficult and dangerous tasks.

Nat Palmer was an obvious choice for the job. Not yet of age, he received his first deep-sea command: the sloop *Hero.* She had been built in 1800 in Groton, not far from Stonington.

Yachtsmen in this century have felt proud of themselves when they crossed the Atlantic in a staunch new 80-footer with auxiliary power. Modern shipowners would not dream of sending any craft of less than 1000 tons on a long voyage. We can get an idea of the spirit of young America from the fact that no-one seems to have considered it very remarkable, in 1820, that a vessel 47 feet 3 inches long should be sent on a direct voyage of some 9000 miles or more, to the edge of the Antarctic, under the command of a youngster who could celebrate his own and the sloop's coming of age during the voyage itself. If twenty was young for a deep-sea skipper, it was old for a deep-sea sloop.

The beam of the *Hero* was 16 feet 10 inches, her depth of hold 6 feet 9 inches. Her tonnage was registered at 44 and $^{40}\!/_{95}$ths. Accurately reported tonnage figures, prior to the middle of the Eighteen Hundreds, generally end in a fraction with 95 as the denominator. The reason may be of interest. The term "tonnage," in rating vessels, expresses cubic feet of stowage capacity rather than pounds. A ton of freight was the amount that would fill forty cubic feet in the hold. As the typical vessel had hardly a straight line in her construction, the tonnage in cubic feet was difficult to measure precisely. Port officers, in computing tonnage fees and other forms of taxes, would have had a tremendous problem in surveying and in solid geometry every time a ship arrived, if they had attempted to figure her precise actual capacity. Yet they were reluctant to trust the tonnage given in the ship's papers, especially if she happened to be of foreign registry. Therefore a fairly simple formula was decided upon, using the vessel's length, breadth, and depth. A full cargo often made the depth difficult to measure. Most old vessels, aft, were deeper but narrower than forward. For these reasons it was decided by rule of thumb, in most ports, to call the depth one-half the breadth. This evidently was not done in the case of the *Hero*, when William Fanning registered her at the Port of New London on July 25th, 1820—as you will see if you care to use the following formula on her dimensions as given above.

$$\text{Tons} = \frac{(\text{Length less } \frac{3}{5} \text{ of breadth}) \times \text{breadth} \times \text{depth}}{95}$$

Oliver Champlain, surveyor of the district, further described her as having one deck, one mast, a square stern, and no galleries.

The *Hero* was a coasting sloop, designed not only to hug the shore but also to run up and down the rivers that were still the only inland freight routes when she was laid down. Although typical for such uses, she was far from usual for deep-water work, as the proportion of her breadth to depth makes clear. In regarding half the beam, for practical measurement, as being equivalent to depth, surveyors were aware that most shipbuilders took advantage of their rule of thumb. Tonnage of a vessel twenty feet broad would be measured as if she were ten feet deep, but the practice usually was to make her twelve or fourteen feet deep. This provided extra stowage space on which no tax had to be paid.

The true reported depth of the *Hero*, however—6 feet 9 inches—was less instead of more than half the breadth of 16 feet 10 inches. This circumstance made it advantageous for her owners to insist that the exact rule be applied in her case. She had not been built to beat the rule. She was a coaster. Coasting vessels paid much lower fees and taxes than others, and they had to be of shallow draft to sail close inshore and up shallow rivers. Both of these facts go to show that the *Hero*, however excellent she might prove as a ferry between ships and shore in the South Shetlands, was a dangerous craft for the long hazardous voyage to her destination. Such shallow lines do well enough in choppy, inshore waters. In long ocean waves they make a vessel exceedingly difficult to handle.

It was an added compliment to Nat Palmer's skill that he should have had allotted to him the task of steering that precarious punkin seed a third of the way around the globe to its destination.

CHAPTER FOURTEEN

WITH PHINEAS WILCOX FOR MATE AND A CREW OF FOUR seamen, Captain Nat Palmer cleared from Stonington on July 31st, 1820. At 6 P.M. they were about twelve miles south and a little to the east of Block Island, from which they took their departure. A vessel does not necessarily take its departure from the port from which it sails. The point of departure, in a technical sense, is more likely to be the last prominent point on the shore, or else an offshore island.

The position of the vessel, once she is out of sight of land, can be found with accuracy by studying heavenly bodies. It can be computed roughly by keeping an account of the direction and the distance she has traveled from the last known point: the point of departure. Captain Palmer, in his first entry in the log book, noted that Block Island was NNW ½ W by compass from the *Hero*, distant about four leagues. He placed a ruler on his chart and pricked a pinhole at that point. Thereafter he kept track of his position by laying the ruler against the last point recorded, slanting it on the chart at the same angle with the meridians as that which the compass showed the sloop to have sailed in the meanwhile, and measuring along the ruler a distance equivalent on the scale of the chart to that recorded by the hourly heaving of the log.

Such pinpricks were made every noon, and as often in between as it had proved necessary to change the course. Suitable corrections were allowed for leeway, currents, and the known variations of the compass. Whenever the heavens permitted, the course as plotted on the chart could be corrected by complicated observations for longitude, usually referred to as "lunars." Any day, if the sun was visible at noon, a correction for latitude was possible.

But in bad weather a vessel might have to sail for hundreds of miles by dead reckoning. A careful account of the point of departure and the distance and direction of each "leg" of the course sailed after that was the only means by which a skipper could keep a fair idea of his position at sea.

Five of the eight Stonington vessels sailed as a fleet, but before the first week was out only the schooner *Express* was in sight from the *Hero*. This pair kept in company to the Falklands and thence to Staten Island, near Cape Horn, arriving October 31st. Ten days later they were sailing amid "penguins, whales, and gulls" of the Antarctic, and on November 12th they found the *Hersilia* at Ragged

Island. Captain Sheffield was able then to tell them of the location of some other vessels of the fleet, which had divided up to give individual attention to various islands of the South Shetland group.

Skins had not yet been gathered in numbers sufficient to require the services of the *Hero* as a lighter to carry them off from the shore. Consequently it was decided to send her on further explorations. Later accounts imply that from a high lookout on one of the islands a suspicion of land much farther to the south was seen. Credit has been given for the first glimpse of it to both Captain Pendleton and to Palmer himself. Captain Edmund Fanning's account, published in 1833, says "it appeared" from Captain Pendleton's report that he had seen an active volcano far in the south from a high lookout on Deception Island. This obviously was a misreading, on Fanning's part, of what really "appeared" in Pendleton's story. The facts in the log books kept by both Pendleton and his youngest subordinate captain show clearly that Palmer, three days after his arrival at President Harbor, was sent by Pendleton to look for more rookeries. Palmer wrote in his log, on November 15th, "stood over for Deception, course E for the north head." He then definitely explored the coast, looking for a harbor and recording the search in terms which make it plain that the Stonington sealers did not previously know of the internal peculiarities of that island.

The logbook of the *Hero*, now in the Library of Congress, shows that on November 16th Palmer ran out of a snowstorm almost into the mouth of a wonderful harbor. The entrance was narrow—less than a cable's length, or 600 feet, in width. Inside, the rock walls expanded in a great circle five miles in diameter. Jets of steam, drifting upward all around the harbor's edge, proved it to be the cone of a sunken volcano, with a fissure in the eastern rim conveniently provided for the entry of mariners.

A volcano fizzing steam at the edges might not seem the safest of havens. But to men who had been buffeted by Antarctic icy gales, and who had recently been blinded by a blizzard, the evidences of warmth aroused more satisfaction than apprehension. Yankee Harbor, as it presently was named, was soon to be the favorite anchorage of the sealing fleet. But at this time Pendleton, it seems clear, knew nothing of it, for he would certainly have told the master of the exploring sloop all he did know that would aid in making the expedition efficient. Thus Pendleton could not, as Fanning claims, have been on a high point of Deception Island without having discovered that Deception Island was what Palmer first found it to be: a C-shaped volcano rim.

After a brief inspection, the *Hero* put to sea again and headed due south toward the suspicion of land which obviously Palmer himself must have seen from the lookout on Deception Island. The better part of a day's sailing brought him and his crew near high and desolate mountains. They were looking for seal rookeries, and as the black rocks and vast glaciers of the new land became clearer, it is to be doubted that they thought of it as anything more notable than another mountainous island or series of islands, similar to the South Shetlands themselves. They must have thought too of the lost Auroras. But the eyes focusing anxiously on the coast itself failed to discover what they most sought: seals.

Off the mouth of a channel choked with ice, and trending a little south of west between two peaks, Nat Palmer shot the sun and recorded the latitude as 63° 45′. This was at noon on November 18th, 1820. After lingering a few days to make sure that there were no seals, Palmer cruised northward again directly to Ragged Island to report.

The only immediate result of this cruise was the removal of several vessels of the Stonington fleet to a situation where they might literally sit on a volcano, in the great harbor of Deception Island.

Columbus sought the East Indies by sailing west. Discovering instead merely a new world, he was at first perplexed and disappointed. Nat Palmer, the only other certain discoverer of a continent whose name is known to us, was looking for seals. He seems to have thought nothing of it when, in a sloop of about the same tonnage as the smallest of Columbus' fleet, he voyaged alone into more perilous seas than Columbus ever encountered, and became the first shipmaster to touch at the mainland of Antarctica. Only one explorer before, in the history of the world, had sailed nearer the south pole: Captain Cook, R.N., had gone seven or eight degrees farther, in the Pacific side. Having found in that locality only pack ice, Cook had returned to make the report still generally credited in Nat Palmer's youth: that geographers' dreams of an Antarctic continent were dreams and nothing more.

The sloop *Hero* reached President Harbor in Ragged Island on November 21st, and sailed with several vessels of the fleet to the new rendezvous in the volcano. For more than a month thereafter she was constantly employed freighting supplies to the camps in various islands of the

South Shetlands, and in lightering off the sealskins to the brigs. President Harbor had been abandoned as an anchorage after one of the brigs had nearly been driven aground there and lost, but it remained the best rookery. Most of the *Hero's* voyages thus continued to be between Ragged and Deception Islands.

Vessels from other ports, both in England and North America, began to arrive in uncomfortable numbers. There was some unpleasantness between the rival crews. The typical arrangement called for payment of the crew in shares from the final proceeds of the voyage. Each man consequently had a personal reason for trying to get to a new herd ahead of his rivals. One result of these energetic activities was to drive the dwindling, remaining herds away. In January conditions had become so difficult that Nat Palmer was sent again to explore the new land he had discovered, to see whether seals had reached it in the interval.

This time he followed a coast that trended southwesterly for more than 300 miles from the point at which he had originally touched. He drew a careful map, the first ever made of the Antarctic continent. But he found no seals.

Returning to the South Shetlands, Palmer then explored and mapped the more difficult straits and bays of those islands. Early in the morning of February 6th, 1812, he was lying to in a dense fog amongst icebergs, waiting for the weather to clear. At half past midnight he struck one bell, and heard an answering chime which he thought was an echo from an ice island. At one o'clock, when he struck two bells, these also seemed to be answered.

Every half hour the response was heard, with enough variation in time and loudness to make the theory of an echo more doubtful. The Antarctic sun, circling low around the horizon, but rising somewhat higher as it swept past the east and northward, finally began to burn through the fog. Phineas Wilcox, who had replaced his skipper on watch at eight bells, or four o'clock in the morning, called him again at seven. Two or three hours later they were discussing the bells, the mate calling them "tricky," and regarding them as some special natural phenomenon, when they thought they heard voices and the plop and drip of oars.

As the fog suddenly lifted, they were prepared to see evidence of a rival sealer. Instead, close on the lee quarter of the *Hero*, they saw a ship's boat manned by neatly attired naval men. In the stern sheets sat an officer who wore a foreign uniform they did not recognize. A little farther off a sloop-of-war was lying. On the other quarter they could make out the white belt and black gun ports of a frigate. The fog swirled higher, disclosing the imperial colors of the empire farthest away of any in the world: Russia.

The officer climbed over the *Hero's* low gunwale and into the waist, where he announced to Captain Palmer that his presence was requested aboard His Russian Majesty's Frigate *Vostok*. Palmer stepped into the boat, and a few minutes later was walking aft on the deck of the frigate.

Awaiting him in the great cabin he found a group of officers in their dress uniforms. The commander of the expedition arose and introduced himself as Captain Faddei Faddeyevitch Ballingshausen. The visitor, clad in sealskin jacket and boots, said his name was Palmer and that he came from Stonington in the U. S. A.

Explaining that the two corvettes were on an official exploring expedition for Tsar Alexander, the commander asked information concerning the land in sight to the northward.

"They are the South Shetlands," Palmer told him. "If you wish to visit any of them, it will afford me pleasure to be your pilot."

The Russian thanked him, and admitted regretfully that a previous glimpse of the land through the mist had led him to believe he had made a new discovery. He had sailed from Europe before the return of the *Hersilia* to Stonington had revealed the location of the South Shetlands to the world. It must have been a little annoying, to a famous explorer forty-two years of age, when a youth of twenty-one offered to pilot him along the intricacies of what he until a few moments before had thought to be with one exception the most inaccessible land on the map.

Ballingshausen himself, a month or so earlier, had crept south toward a wall of ice and had sighted an island near the edge of it, in latitude 69°, but it had appeared small and ice-locked. He had not ventured over the pack ice to investigate. It was the only land he had seen, that could surely be identified as land and not ice, in over a year of sailing zigzags around the bottom of the world.

When Palmer mentioned, in reply to another question, that he knew of more extensive land still farther south, the Russian explorer arose in much concern and insisted that logbook and chart be produced to verify the statement. Young Captain Palmer complied. While these were being sent for, luncheon was served.

Presently the logbook and chart were spread on the

table. Ballingshausen studied them and was satisfied. He apparently was so much impressed by the accuracy of the survey that he thought it both unfair and impertinent to do the job over again. Instead, he stood away to the north and east, leaving to Nat Palmer himself the privilege of informing the world of his discovery.

Ballingshausen dutifully completed his full circuit of the south polar regions, missing a number of other islands that were soon to be discovered by Nat Palmer. The Russian had penetrated, in the open sea, a little farther south than anyone else but Cook, and had called a stretch of ice Alexander Land, on the off chance that land might lie beyond it. It did, at a distance of nearly a hundred miles, a later verified fact which classes it with the valid hunches rather than the true discoveries. But the most notable historical result of his voyage was the proof his journal gives that a boy from Connecticut, in a sloop the size of the *Vostok's* launch, thought nothing of having found what geographers had dreamt of and mapped by imagination for two centuries.

Nat Palmer had been looking for seals. Continents were of no use to him, if they had no rookeries in view.

CHAPTER FIFTEEN

I HAVE EMPHASIZED THE EARLY CAREER OF N. B. PALMER, at a time when it had no particular connection with the forces that were shaping up toward the clipper ships, because we need occasional reminders that a machine is no more useful or capable than the human brain that operates it. The great days of the clippers were made possible only by the great seamen who drove them as no other whole class of ships has ever been driven. To understand the achievements of the ships, we need first to know the spirit of the men on the quarterdeck.

Hard stories have been told of the brutalities on board some clippers, and of the hardships that were taken for granted on all of them. Many of the tales are true. Wisdom was not operating in all departments of the shipping business. It seems to have occurred to nobody, in the old sailing ship days, that it would have been sensible in the long run to give common seamen decent quarters to live in, reasonable working hours, and a larger part of the profits of good voyages. Owners claimed that they could not afford it, and pointed to the bankruptcies of shipping men by way of proof. But successful ones pocketed great sums of money some of the time, whereas the poor devil of a common seaman was getting no more—in terms of what his money could buy—in boom days than he was when times were hard.

One reason, I suppose, was the memory the great commanders had of their own early days in subordinate positions. Instead of trying to better the conditions of their common seamen they thanked the school of hard knocks for their own later virtues. Nat Palmer never had a reputation as a "bucko" among his men, but even he was probably inclined to look back on months spent among Antarctic blizzards and icebergs, in the heatless cabin of a tiny sloop, as a period beside which the hard times of the average merchant fo'c's'le were not worth complaining about. Such men also said, and wrote in their memoirs, that if an American remained a drunken common sailor it was his own business. Pity should not be wasted upon him. Those who wished could quickly rise to command. And so they could, at most times during the period between the Revolution and the Civil War. After that the decline of the American merchant marine began, and many a man who had been a captain was glad of a job as second mate.

But in Nat Palmer's days, the great days of our maritime

history, expansion was almost continuous, and opportunities offered in a dozen directions at once.

The *Hero* left Yankee Harbor for Stonington on February 14th, 1821, and arrived April 29th. In less than three months young Nat was off for Antarctica again as skipper of the *James Monroe*, a sloop about twice the size of the *Hero*. His job continued to be that of hunting for new seal rookeries to be exploited by larger vessels of the Stonington fleet. In the course of his duties he sailed for a third time to his Antarctic continent, on this occasion to explore the shoreline eastward. When forced off by continuous stretches of pack ice which gave no hope of seals, he stood northward to Elephant Island, one of the more easterly of the South Shetlands, and there chanced to encounter a young British sealer: Captain Powell of the sloop *Dove*.

The two seem to have liked and to have trusted each other. Sailing in company on an impromptu exploring expedition farther toward the east, they came upon a large group of islands which they named after Powell. Most maps now indicate them as the South Orkneys. These too the unfortunate Ballingshausen, by an ill-inspired reach to the northward, had managed not to encounter.

Powell, upon return of the two sloops to the anchorage in Yankee Harbor, asked for and received the charts of all the sealers. From these the first detailed map of the region was made up and published a year later. It shows by name both Powell's Group and Palmer's Land. Even earlier a map of the entire Western Hemisphere had been published in Hartford, Connecticut, accurately locating and naming Palmer's Land. These facts are important because credit for what was really Palmer's discovery has been claimed instead for later explorers. But the first maps name the land after the man who found it, and indicate the shoreline with enough precision to prove that he explored it with care.

Nat Palmer may not have appreciated the importance of his discovery in 1820, but by 1822 he was aware that it was not just another island. On his return from the voyage in which he had made his third visit to the mainland of Antarctica he was interviewed by the *New London Gazette*, which printed a story in the issue of April 24th, 1822, beginning: "We have been favored with interesting particulars respecting a *Southern Continent*, by Capt. Nathaniel B. Palmer."

The story, after a description of the exploration, ends: "There is now no doubt, that there exists a *South Continent* . . ."

What no longer existed, in the regions southeast of Cape Horn, was a herd of seals worth the hunting. Once more the remorseless butchery had ruined the business for all concerned. Captain Nat turned from sealing for the time being to an occupation perhaps as hazardous in a different way. His orders for the last voyage home, received from Captain Pendleton January 25th, 1822, advised him to have "as little communication with the main as possible."

South America was up in arms. Bolivar had already succeeded in freeing a large part of it from Spain, but the struggle was continuing. Conditions of anarchy in many ports made it impossible to guess what sort of reception a Yankee would receive. He might be plundered by either faction, in the name of necessity, or pressed into service with his vessel in the cause of whichever side saw him first.

Nat Palmer, having obediently gone home without any communication with the South American mainland, promptly turned around and sailed in command of another vessel to the island of St Bartholomew on the rim of the privateer- and pirate-haunted Spanish Main. He seems to have taken the dangerous jobs by preference, in this period. We next learn of him as master of the schooner *Cadet*, ferrying arms and recruits for Bolivar from Panama to Colombia, and taking gangs of prisoners over to Cuba. The *Cadet* was wrecked while under his command, a fact not held against him as he soon was given the brig *Tampico*. In 1827 he married Eliza Thompson Babcock of Stonington. By 1828 he had become owner of his brig.

Next year he sailed in command of the *Annawan* on an exploring expedition financed by the Fannings. During this voyage he was captured by escaped convicts on Juan Fernandez who were dissuaded from shooting him only by one of their own number who belonged to the same secret society as Captain Nat. The adventures in connection with this episode can be found in John R. Spears' biography of Palmer, which however should not be trusted in some portions concerning the Antarctic episodes.

While the *Annawan*, Captain Palmer, was on a second voyage in the South Seas, a pair of very notable events occurred in the history of American naval architecture. The firm of S. & F. Fickett laid down the ship *Huntsville*, and the neighboring rival firm of Webb & Allen began to build at almost the same time the almost identical ship *Natchez*. Both were designed specifically as New Orleans packets. Three others, very similar in dimensions but less famous in performance, also were built in New York during the year

1831. All five had a marked peculiarity of construction which makes it something of a puzzle to account for the fact that they were originally produced for different owners.

At that time, packet lines had been operating between New York and New Orleans for about ten years, applying to coastal shipping the principle of continuous ownership which had proved so successful in the case of the pioneer ocean packet service, the Black Ball line to Liverpool organized in New York in 1816. Unlike the Black Ballers and their increasingly numerous rivals in the trade to Europe, the New Orleans lines did not at first attempt to keep to a regular schedule of sailings, full or empty, fair weather or foul. But groups of owners associated with one another to keep the ships going on a schedule suited to the seasonal production of the principal commodity carried: cotton.

Speed characterized the New Orleans packet service from the beginning. Cotton, the chief cargo, was not perishable. We can probably call it a symptom of the growing belief that the surest route to more profits was to make more complete voyages a year. The early cotton carriers, as a consequence, were usually designed according to the best current theories concerning speed. They had V-shaped bottoms, with a considerable drag aft.

Both of these features tended to reduce the possible stowage space very greatly. As the production of cotton increased, and the demand for more ships brought new competitors into the packet service, the size of the individual vessels also was enlarged. The original ones measured around 250 tons. By the middle Eighteen Twenties the new vessels were averaging over 400 tons. One result of the steady increase in size, as a glance at the features of

sharp floor and after drag will prove,[1] was the early necessity to modify the mould if the bigger ships were to be able
to cross the mud and sandbars that forever were building
up anew at the mouth of the Mississippi. Dredging on a
large scale was not yet thought feasible. The only other
thing to do was to make the larger ships shallower in proportion.

A succession of annoying but not dangerous delays, with
ships stranded on the bars and costly bills for warping them
off again, convinced the owners that sharp models built for
speed were not worth having if they spent a day or more
each voyage with their after drags wedged in the mud and
sand of the delta. The practical logic of the Mississippi
delta persuaded ship designers that it would make better
sense to reduce the drag aft and increase the depth of the
useful hold forward.

Keels flattened out noticeably toward a horizontal line
during the Eighteen Twenties, and the sharpness of floor
began to be reduced too. None of these factors, however,
account for the sudden decision of different owners, in
1831, to contract almost simultaneously for five ships in
which the change of design was so pronounced that there
seems to have been a general agreement to give up the
idea of speed.

The new ships, typified by the *Huntsville* and *Natchez*,
were meant to carry cotton bales and they were built like
a cotton bale. Instead of attempting to get speed with a
V-shaped floor and a long, narrow run aft which could
carry no cargo at all, they were nearly flat in the mid section, and the flatness carried farther forward and aft than

[1] See illustrations on page 212.

even the gentler bulge of the earlier types of convoy ships had done. Only in one particular were the *Huntsville*, *Natchez, Nashville, Louisville,* and *Creole* evidently aiming at speed. Their ratio of length to beam was 4.4 to 1. They thus were relatively longer and narrower than even the United States naval vessels of their own time.

Was there some particular event, the publication of a very persuasive argument, or a change in harbor fees, behind the sudden and almost unanimous decision of several New York builders and owners to change so remarkably the general character of the New Orleans packets? So far I have been unable to find what it was. Did others decide to copy quickly the lines of the first of these ships, to make sure that a rival would not steal a march? If so, the fact is in itself remarkable. It was the general tendency of American builders to make no two ships alike.

It may have been merely the desire of each set of owners to match their rivals' ships in size. In doing only that, they would have known that the current tendency to flatten the floor and the run must be carried to its final extreme, if their bigger ships were to get over the river bars. Then too, it may mark a general realization on the part of all concerned that if ships were to be owned and operated continuously in "lines" it was time to break away from the old average type, which could be sold at the end of the voyage to anybody for any trade, and to begin making instead a type of vessel suited to an exacting trade with a particular port.

Whatever caused the change, the fleet of new cotton ships surprised everybody by making voyages a bit faster, on the average, than those of their predecessors. The main reason, however, seems to have been overlooked at first. Obviously, the ships were larger and narrower. Other things being equal, size had long been known to contribute to speed. Yankees had definitely proved to themselves, if not yet to the world at large, that narrower models could be so designed as to stand up and use the wind to best advantage. At first it was thought that these two factors had more than made up for the assumed loss of speed caused by the flat floor.

The new ships, although they were fuller in the after body, retained the apple-cheeked appearance forward that had been characteristic of cargo carriers from the beginning of time. After they had been operated for a few voyages, a particularly enterprising young shipowner named Edward K. Collins saw which way the wind was blowing and organized the ownership of the five vessels more tightly into a single operating company, although each ship as formerly was owned by several shareholders.

Collins, perhaps more than any other shipping figure, typifies the trait which was rapidly making the United States the most important of maritime nations: a willingness to gamble on what seemed to be the new and better thing, in the belief that trade and profits would follow the leader. One of his first moves, after he got control of the Louisiana and New York Line, was to sign up on a semipermanent basis the most enterprising shipmasters he could find.

Collins may have heard about Nat Palmer through a relative, Amos Palmer, who was part owner of the *Huntsville* and *Louisville* when they first went into service. At any rate, when he was thirty-five, the discoverer of the

Antarctic mainland was given command of his first packet, the *Huntsville.* Her "operator" was three years younger than that.

Tact, and an ability to get along with all kinds of individuals, were important factors in the packet trade, especially in days when the divergent interests of the North and South were beginning to seem apparent. Captain Palmer had demonstrated his possession of an abundance of both qualities at every point in his career. From his association with the skipper of the *Espirito Santo* (who might well have resented being followed by a youngster to his secret sealing ground) to his Caribbean experiences as commander of a troop ship full of Latin revolutionaries, his record indicates a disposition rare in a man who had seen so much of hardship and brutality in the sealing industry and elsewhere. He was an immediate success as a packet skipper.

After two years of coasting to New Orleans and back, Captain Palmer was sent by Mr Collins to Liverpool on a mission of private diplomacy that was another tribute to the wide range of his abilities. Having conquered the cotton trade, the restless and ambitious young shipowner had decided to force his way into the most exacting but also the most profitable of maritime fields: the "Rail Road Route to Europe." To do so, he had to make the proper commercial connections in a terminal port on the other side, and to secure the substantial backing of English agents. Instead of going himself, his usual procedure when anything of importance was to be done, Collins showed his confidence in the best of his shipmasters by sending Captain Nat.

CHAPTER SIXTEEN

SAILING SHIP MEN SPOKE OF THE ATLANTIC OCEAN AS IF it went uphill in one direction, downhill in the other. From Europe to America was the uphill passage. The reason lay in the prevailing habit of the winds. Typical North Atlantic gales were westerlies, blowing toward Europe. Ships sailing toward the United States had to buck the winds more often than not, tacking most of the way. In the early days of the service, the average packet ship run from New York to Liverpool, dock to dock, was three and a half weeks. The return voyage, uphill, normally required five and a half weeks. These averages were considerably reduced as ships became larger but narrower in proportion.

The always difficult uphill passage was worst in winter,

when English shipowners were reluctant to send their vessels to America at all. Westerly passages requiring more than two months were common, in that worst season. The cost of such a voyage, in wages and damage to the top-hamper, frequently canceled off the possibility of profits. Growing cities of the Atlantic seaboard began to regard this seasonal variation in ship arrivals as a distinct annoyance. Americans sent their own ships more and more into the winter trade. At first there was no concerted plan. Periods of many weeks still were experienced when no vessels at all arrived from Europe. At such times, all workers and merchants who made their livelihood from the handling of incoming cargoes were idle.

Four New York merchants decided to do something about it. Instead of regarding one another as rivals to be outwitted, they pooled their resources and four of their ships to establish the first commercial packet line. Parts of their original advertisement of October 27th, 1817, are significant:

> "It is the intention of the owners that one of these vessels shall sail from New-York on the 5th and one from Liverpool on the 1st of every month.
>
> "These ships have all been built in New-York, of the best materials, and are coppered and copper fastened. They are known to be remarkably fast sailers. . . .
>
> "The commanders of them are all men of great experience and activity; and they will do all in their power to render these Packets eligible conveyances for passengers. It is also thought, that the regularity of

their times of sailing, and the excellent condition in which they deliver their cargoes, will make them very desirable opportunities for the conveyance of goods."

It proved impossible to make the new line's English agents take seriously, at first, the unheard-of principle that a ship should sail at the advertised hour, whether or not she was loaded, and despite the condition of the weather. The first sailing, supposed to be from Liverpool on the auspicious January 1st of a new year, was postponed three days despite rigid instructions. But the *James Monroe*, 424 tons, cast off her lines from the New York pier at 10 A.M. on January 5th, 1818, precisely as advertised, which was all the more dramatic because the men laying aloft to shake the canvas out of its gaskets had to scoop great mounds of snow from the yards in the process of finding a grip. Before the little vessel—a notably big one she seemed in her day—had progressed very far down the East River she was blanketed from sight by the blinding snow.

The cruelest winter in years gave the determination of the packet sponsors a thorough test. New York Harbor froze solid in February, but the second Black Baller to sail eastward got away on time, and in the nick of time, before the freeze. When the March sailing also went off on schedule, despite foul weather, the Black Ball Line had proved itself in the eyes of the public.

Four years later the success of the new principle of regular sailings was attested beyond a doubt by the competition of another line, the Red Star, with sailings on the 25th of the month, blow high, blow low, full or empty. The Black Ballers replied to that by adding four more ships and increasing their scheduled sailings to two a month. In mid-summer of the same year, 1822, the Swallowtail Line appeared, to prove that the response to the new Yankee idea was so great that there was room for yet another. Thereafter, throughout sixteen years, the packets kept scrupulously to the same schedule of sailing dates except in times of public calamity such as the great waterfront fires. These exceptions were exceedingly infrequent. New Yorkers came to rely without question on the fact that a Black Baller would sail on the first of the month, a Swallowtail on the 8th, another Black Baller on the 16th, and a Red Star on the 24th. It was a new idea in the world, and for decades it was done only in America.

Business followed the daring gamble. The regular liners charged, and got, premium prices for their freight. Travelers were willing to pay higher passage rates for sailing in ships which were so reliable that one's affairs could be arranged to the day and hour without a hitch, so far as departure was concerned, with arrival also predictable to a degree never before dreamt of.

The contrast can be appreciated by those who have read Benjamin Franklin's account of going aboard a "packet" (in the old sense of the word) which frittered away six weeks inside Sandy Hook, after all the passengers were aboard, waiting for dispatches which a Royal Governor was slow in preparing. Speedy sailing did not really become important until speedy departure also was assured.

Lines to London and Le Havre soon were in operation, in addition to those to Liverpool. Coastal packets, less regular in their schedules, also were organized into lines in the eighteen twenties, such as the ones to New Orleans mentioned in the last chapter.

It may seem curious that all of the commercial backing of a service equally important to Great Britain and the United States should have come from the American side, especially when it is recalled that the Revolutionary War was largely fought over the stubborn desire of British shipowners to monopolize the American carrying trade.

The profits which lured more and more shipowners of New York, Philadelphia, and Boston into the establishment of packet lines must have been as obvious an inducement to their British cousins. Yet there is no record of a serious British attempt at competition until the coming of the steamship lines, twenty years and more after the Yankee packets had become well established.

The usual reason given is British conservatism, but it is not a good enough one, unless the meaning of the word is expanded and made clear. I shall attempt to do that in the next chapter.

But there was a growing disposition at least to cooperate, in Liverpool. Captain Nat Palmer brought back, toward the end of the year 1835, a report that E. K. Collins should have little difficulty in earning dividends with still another line of packets to that port. Collins had done exceedingly well with his New Orleans line, and intended to take no half measures with the Liverpool one. His best New Orleans ship, the *Shakespeare*, formed the nucleus of the new group. She seems to have been the inspiration for the line's name, unless Collins had named the *Shakespeare* herself, a year earlier, with plans for the Dramatic Line already well in mind.

To the *Shakespeare* he proposed to add three other vessels named after famous personages connected with the stage. His determination to divert a typical cotton ship to the Atlantic route seemed foolish to many. Five years after the building of the *Huntsville* and the *Nashville*, their success was still being ascribed mainly to narrowness and hard driving. General opinion still had it that if it were not for their flat floors they would be even faster.

Nat Palmer thought differently. Approving the idea of putting the *Shakespeare* on the European run, he went further, and assured Collins that the flat floor which had been provided merely to let the cotton ships get over the bars actually was the main secret of their speed. Having sailed for two years in the similarly flat-floored *Huntsville*, he could claim that his belief was the product of experience.

Although Palmer won his point at the moment, and convinced Collins, the argument was to continue for a great while longer before shipbuilders in general were won over. One reason was the curious fact, still unexplained, that the other three ships of the flat-floored quintuplets of 1831, the *Nashville*, *Creole*, and *Louisville*, averaged four days longer per passage than the *Natchez* and *Huntsville*, and were thus no faster than the older packets of the Eighteen Twenties.

Another reason why the argument continued was the almost too great brilliance of a young man of twenty-seven who himself was engaged in the same job of dreaming the perfect ship into life. This dreamer, a draftsman named Griffiths, was about to give to shipbuilding the scientific spirit which it had never systematically commanded before.

He was going to succeed so well with a combination of two main principles, which appeared in all his models, that even he himself was not to discover the faults of one of them until some years later.

John Willis Griffiths had not yet got a hearing. Nathaniel Brown Palmer, with a growing reputation for achievement and common sense as well as all kinds of experience to draw from, had less difficulty in convincing the young financial wizard, Collins. Brown & Bell, who were commissioned to build the nearly identical *Garrick* and *Sheridan* for the Dramatic Line in 1836, were appalled by the possible effect upon their reputation of the principle which Palmer, through Collins, insisted upon expressing in the new liners. There were no sandbars that need bother a competent skipper, between the East River piers and the King's dock in Liverpool. Why in the world then, Brown and his partner Bell wondered, should the two splendid new ships be handicapped with flat floors?

Nat Palmer had the answer. In the flat-floored *Huntsville* he had come around from New Orleans in ten days, faster than any other ship had ever made the run. His average for all runs in her had been fifteen days, compared with nineteen or twenty for the rest of the cotton fleet.

But there was a type of mind very prevalent in South Street that would make the response: "If she weren't flat-floored you'd have done it faster than that. Look at the *Creole*. She was flat-floored, and your people got rid of her, she was so slow."

There was only one answer to such an argument: "Try it and see." Everyone admitted that the best merchant ships in the world were already in service in the Black Ball

Line. They were fairly sharp-bottomed. If a flat-floored ship could beat them, that would be the best answer.

Young Donald McKay, a journeyman shipwright employed in several of the East River yards at this period, probably turned a puzzled, Nova Scotian eye toward such a pair of curiosities on the stocks as the *Garrick* and the *Sheridan*. McKay was never hurried in his decisions. He had the sort of all-devouring mind that accepts millions of facts and allows them to churn around slowly until some rise as froth and some sink, the rest jostling one another and continuing the process until a balanced form composed only of the best floats in the clear middle region of the inner vision.

Griffiths and McKay later were friends. One of McKay's grandsons has written of his belief that they early discussed together the principles of naval architecture. If so, the case of the two Dramatic packets could hardly have escaped them. In any discussion of the merits of sharp floor versus flat floor, at that time, Griffiths surely would have taken up the cudgels against Nat Palmer's idea.

Whatever way the possible arguments may have gone, one enormously important thing had happened. The threads of influence that had grown from many different places, by trial and error, by inspiration and luck, at last were gathering closely together. Events that had built fore castles and razed them again, that had first made lateen sails and centuries later had split the jib from the rest, were converging within one city. The accumulated principles learned from naval warfare and blockades were being caught up in the enterprising spirit that had driven Nat Palmer to the edge of the Antarctic continent. They were caught up as well in the different, balancing urge that had led John Griffiths toward new conquests of the mind. The three individual men who were to contribute most toward making the world's most wonderful ships at last had been brought together on one small stretch of South Street in the city of New York.

All were young. Nat Palmer, the eldest, was thirty-seven, Griffiths ten years younger. McKay, the youngest, was twenty-six. Their achievements came along in the same order. Yet it is well to remember that the rivalry of the Rail Road Route to Europe was necessary to give a real chance either to the dreamers or to the men who said, "Try it and see." On that wild Atlantic Shuttle, speed had become increasingly the test of success. Business swung mainly to the line that hung up the best speed records for others to shoot at.

In earlier days, a vessel had stayed at her pier until she was full. The first merchant to get his freight aboard might sit back for weeks while others were being signed up to take the remaining space. "For prompt dispatch," was always the sign in the rigging, but "prompt" had a very elastic meaning until the competing packet lines established weekly sailings. Under the new system, the average merchant could complete his deal and recover his investment with profit in half the time or less, compared with the old days. Twice the number of yearly deals made twice as much money from the same amount of capital. That was why speed appealed to the merchants of New York, and why they were eager to pay extra for it.

They were willing to pay so much extra, in fact, that on the day when Nat Palmer graduated from the New Orleans service to the Liverpool run he had every reason to look forward to riches. His salary was $30 a month, but this was dwarfed by the percentage he received of the freight and passage money. On the basis of Spears' estimates, Captain Nat on a single typical run would have received $200 as his share of the freight money, and $2100 from the fares paid by passengers, to say nothing of the very considerable fees for carrying letters. Eight runs a year were normal— four round voyages. A successful packet captain thus could look forward with some confidence to $20,000 a year. That, in the Eighteen Thirties and Forties, was a huge amount.

No doubt the men who got it earned it. The performance of a Western Ocean packet liner was generally dependent upon one man, the captain. To maintain the reputation of his ship and line, to say nothing of himself, he had to stay on deck almost constantly from land to land, driving his men to utter exhaustion, but driving himself most of all. The worse the weather, the more important it became for the old man to keep his place on the quarter-deck.

There were dead-of-winter voyages when the great packet skippers refused throughout to go below for more than five minutes at a time—never to sleep. They slept lashed to a chair, literally, with one eye half open and wits ready to respond to those sensitive little indicators with which a sailing ship is crowded: the chirrup of sheaves that could stand a greater strain than they evidently were getting, or at the other extreme, the groan of a spar wrenched to the limit of endurance, a groan that could turn into a splintering crack and crash if the wind should step up its pace ever so little.

It was the skipper's business almost to drive the sticks out of her: almost, but not quite. No subordinate dared risk his less secure position by carrying sail so continuously near to the edge of catastrophe. That was why the old man could not sleep below, if he wanted a record run.

It was on such a voyage that Captain Nat, on the blustery first of November, 1837, left New York in command of the new *Garrick*. On the same tide sailed the *England*, commanded by Ben Waite. No circumstances could have been provided for a better test. The *England*, a Black Baller only three years old, was at that moment probably the most famous ship in the line. Her captain was a superman who throve on hardship, and was delighted with the chance to pit his sharp-bottomed ship against so odd an upstart as the flat-floored *Garrick*.

The two ships arrived in Liverpool on the 17th, ending the race almost neck and neck. But the *Garrick* had been off Cape Clear in twelve days, the fastest passage on record to that Irish turning post. The rivals sailed almost together on the return voyage, with Waite confident that if the big flat-floored ship could keep up with him running before the wind, the uphill passage home with the wind in their teeth would be a very different story. But again the two ships raced neck and neck, arriving off Sandy Hook within a few hours of each other.

If this impromptu race did not prove the superiority of the flat floor, it at least proved that there was nothing wrong with it. By 1839 the Dramatic liners, including the *Siddons*, a new sister ship of the *Garrick* and *Sheridan*, as well as the larger *Roscius*, had averaged faster passages to westward than any other line. Captain Nat, in the *Siddons*, had sailed the fastest ship in our navy almost hull down in ten hours.

Hardly a packet was built, that year, which did not take advantage of Nat Palmer's discovery that the flat floor contributed to fast sailing. Captain Charles H. Marshall, veteran skipper of the Black Ball Line, summed the matter up when he wrote the following comment at the end of the Eighteen Thirties:

"During my being in the line from 1822 to 1832, I do not think the models of the ships were much changed; but they were increased in size. The general impression then among merchants, and even among nautical men, was that to produce fast sailing it was necessary to build the ships with sharp bottoms, by giving them much *dead rise* and consequently abridging their carrying qualities. It has been found, however, that our predecessors were altogether mistaken in their notions of gaining speed by *dead rise*; it has such a tendency to increase the draft of water, as to produce no speed! It was no uncommon occurrence for a ship of 400 tons to have, in those days, 26 inches *dead rise*. The present models are altogether changed. Our largest ship, say the *Cambridge*, has about 17 inches *dead rise* and were I to build again, I would reduce it to 12 inches. The effect of this is to give buoyancy, and with fine ends so as to secure good steering, the ship will evidently go faster through the water. I should not be surprised if this model were to be adopted for vessels of war.

"The packets that have been built during the last

few years are much greater carriers than those formerly built. They are not only larger but much fuller bodied, caused by less *dead rise*; preserving, however, the same sharpness at each end, and are much *faster* sailers, more comfortable, have less motion, and are much better sea boats."

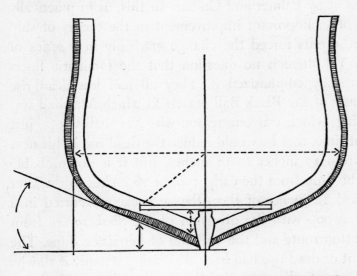

"Dead rise," as used in the captain's letter, referred to the sharpness of the ship's bottom along her keel. In the accompanying illustration, the angle represented by the curved arrows corresponds to the extent of the dead rise, but it was usually measured in inches at a point half-way between the keel and the outside of the largest frame. When the ship was afloat, approximately the same measurement in inches could be got by cutting a rod half as wide as the vessel, laying it crosswise on the inside of the planking, and measuring from it vertically down to the garboard strake beside the keel. A ship with little dead rise was called "flat floored." One with 40" or more of dead rise was rated as "sharp bottomed."

Captain Marshall's letter implies one fact that we should not ignore—his own belief that the change from sharp to flat floor had not come in one sudden decision arrived at by Palmer and Collins. In this, as in practically every other important improvement in the theory of ship design, events forced the change gradually in a series of ships. Yet there is no question that the Dramatic liners dramatically emphasized it. They all had less dead rise than any of the Black Ball vessels to which Marshall was referring, which was one reason why Marshall wrote, just at that time, that he would reduce the dead rise in his next ship from 17 inches to 12 inches. But it is not probable that the drop from the early, typical 26 inches to the later standard 12 inches of the Atlantic packets occurred in a single swoop with the diversion of the *Shakespeare* from the cotton route and the building of her sister ships. The amount of dead rise had been decreasing steadily if slowly. The Dramatic liners carried the trend, rather suddenly, to an extreme.

Captain Nat Palmer, acting as commodore of the Collins Line, took out each of the new Dramatic ships on its first voyage, excepting the *Roscius*. When she was launched, the terrific strain of the Atlantic Shuttle, weeks of constant alertness each voyage with seldom an hour's consecutive sleep, had undermined even the oak and iron constitution of that great shipmaster and he had gone down to his favorite port of call, New Orleans, for a rest. Yet the fact that Collins had given him the honor of first voyage in all the others, and doubtless would have in the case of the *Roscius* too, bears out the testimony which comes from several quarters that Palmer, if he did not actually carve the models, at least had worked so closely in co-operation with the builders that it was his obvious first right to make first trial of the result.

CHAPTER SEVENTEEN

THE YEAR 1822 SAW THE ESTABLISHMENT OF THE RED Star, Second Black Ball, and Swallowtail lines of packets to Liverpool. It is certainly more than a coincidence that in 1823 a committee was appointed in the British Parliament to study ways and means of relieving British shipbuilders from the tonnage restrictions which were beginning to be blamed for the slowness and bad handling qualities of typical British merchantmen. The original Black Ball line no doubt had been regarded as a crack-brained Yankee gesture. But when two competing lines appeared, and when the original one doubled its number of ships and sailings, the more alert Englishmen understood the threat to the traditional Ruler of the Waves.

The Parliamentary Committee recommended that a new system of measurement should be used which would show the true cubic contents of every ship, but for nine years Parliament dallied. Another committee, appointed in 1832, made a more careful study of the tonnage laws of all nations, and submitted similar recommendations. Even then, three years were required to drive the sensible change over the desks of the reluctant Tories. Because it affects all progress all the time, the commercial meaning of extreme, or Tory, conservatism needs to be made clear. If free competition made American trading habits "liberal," then the British merchants undoubtedly tended in the opposite direction and were more than usually "conservative" because they had operated for centuries mainly on a system of exclusive rights and grants from the Crown or from Parliament, one man or company being given a "patent" which guaranteed that no-one else but the patentee could trade in certain places. The East India Company was allowed all the trade with China and India, as well as certain other regions in the East. It maintained a private army and navy to protect its right, and the trade was so profitable so long as others could not compete that there was no reason for thinking up new ideas to improve ships and methods.

For many decades, as an example of this inertia, most ships of the East India Company were made to measure 499 tons. It was not the best size for the trade, but British law required that ships of more than 500 tons should carry chaplains. The British clergy were a privileged class, guaranteed good "livings." The cost of paying a chaplain was large enough to hold down the size of the average East Indiaman for a reason that had nothing to do with the efficiency of the service. Similarly, there was the custom of "ships' husbands," men who had a monopoly on the privilege of supplying ships to the East India Company. They were not shipbuilders, as a rule. They were shipowners, who had ships built for the sole purpose of leasing them to the East India Company. The company, by dealing direct with the shipbuilders, could have saved the extra profits which maintained the ships' husbands in a state of very pleasant affluence. But the ships' husbands were shrewd enough to invest their own wealth in shares of the East India Company. This gave them voting rights whenever the policies of the company were being decided upon. Naturally they used their influence to make sure that their comfortable racket was not voted out of existence; and so the rule continued in force, which forbade the company to own the ships it operated.

That was the sort of thing which made it difficult for British merchant shipping to improve itself. It was not just the conservatism of thinking that old ideas were better than new ones: it was monopoly, the intricate jumble of special Tory privileges which added to the cost of everything. This could not be got rid of without endangering the leisure class which had a firm grip on Parliament and held it grimly—conservatives in the sense that they wanted the special monopolies to be continued, lest free competition make it necessary to get rid of the unproductive costs which represented their own fat incomes.

Most nautical historians dispose of the subject by saying that the British could not compete in the Rail Road Route to Europe of the Yankee packet lines because it cost fifteen or twenty dollars more per ton to build wooden ships in

England than in America. It comes to the same thing. Members of the great useless class that did nothing to earn its own living were indirectly supported by all forms of honest work, partly through high taxes in roundabout ways, partly because materials cost more. But they cost more mainly because they were supplied by monopolies that paid many unnecessary salaries and dividends.

When the British, in a state of desperate alarm at the growth of the merchant marine in other countries, finally overthrew in 1849 and 1854 the worst of the antiquated laws that protected such monopolies, they soon began to produce a few speedy little clippers. Ton for ton, these were as good as those which had been produced in America. But the general improvement in English ships was not to come until the American clipper-ship era had ended in commercial depression, with a civil war following too soon to make recovery possible.

As important a factor as any, in restraining Englishmen from improving their ships, undoubtedly was the rule in force until 1836 for measuring tonnage for the purpose of fixing taxes and port charges. The formula used in Great Britain, when the American packet service began, was similar to that in use in America, but simpler:

$$\text{Tons} = \frac{\text{breadth squared} \times \text{inboard length}}{94}$$

In the American formula, the depth was generally assumed to be one-half the breadth. The British, in the same part of their formula, evidently assumed depth to be the same as breadth, for they merely squared the breadth to get the cross-sectional area. The American rule deducted three-fifths of the breadth from the length before multiplying. The English used the full length (inboard) which was generally a larger number. As a result, when an American ship was measured for port fees in England, she sometimes found herself to be twice as large as when she started her voyage, in terms of measurement tons.

Both systems of measurement were silly. In *The Seaman's Friend*, published at the height of the packet-ship period, Dana reported that an American full-built merchant ship of 500 tons would carry 1000 tons of "measurement goods," whereas a sharp-built one of the same legal measurement would carry 750 tons. The English rule in use till 1835 erred in the other direction. The same two "500 ton" ships, carrying 1000 and 750 tons respectively of measurement goods, would both probably have been assessed for a tonnage of 1100 when they reached Liverpool, which would have been nearly half again as much as the true cargo in the case of the sharp one.

This antiquated rule, originated in days when a ton meant a "tun" or cask of wine, and intended to indicate the number of such casks that could be stowed in the hold, had had two obvious results. As breadth was measured on the main deck, there had been a tendency to make the deck narrower than it should have been, with a very pronounced "tumble home" to the top sides.[1] These spread out in the shape of an old-fashioned kettle, making a ship sometimes as much as ten feet wider under water than on deck. The other result was a tendency to get as much depth as possible, in view of the fact that the tonnage rule,

[1] For an illustration of "tumble home" see upper right-hand figure on page 207.

by squaring the width instead of multiplying width by depth, seemed to take it for granted that the depth would be fully as great as the width.

In spite of these things, if we look at the two formulas as they would be applied to a particular case, it becomes apparent that the follow-the-leader historians who say that the tonnage rules hampered the British more than the Americans never have sharpened their pencils to prove it. Undoubtedly the measurement rules had a discouraging influence upon both British and Americans in their efforts to produce better ships, but the penalty in taxes for making better ships was proportionately greater under the American formula than under the British.

Take as an example an extreme instance of the full-bodied merchantman, 100 feet long inboard (110 feet outboard) and 40 feet broad. Her tonnage under the British rule would measure 1702; under the American it would be 724. But if the beam were reduced by 10 feet to give her a touch of speed and weatherliness, her tonnage under the British formula would be reduced by 745, or 43%, whereas under the American system of measurement it would be reduced by 288 tons, or only 39%.

Sacrificing the same amount of cargo space in both cases, the British ship's owners would have saved 4% more of the original tax bill than the American owners, as a result of the change. Moreover, an Act of Parliament in 1835 changed the British system to one that came fairly near to estimating the true cubic contents, whereas the American law was not similarly changed until 1864. During the intervening twenty-nine years, the Americans were more handicapped in this respect than the British. The American tonnage figures were lower than they should have been in the case of full-built ships, but higher in the case of sharp-built ones. Thus, while British ships for those twenty-nine years were being taxed very nearly on their actual carrying capacity, the American law continued to favor full-built ships and to penalize sharp ones.

The clipper *Blue Jacket*, when she was launched in 1854, measured 1790 tons. When she was remeasured under the new American regulations eleven years later, her true tonnage capacity was found to be 1442. The medium clipper *Ocean Rover*, contrariwise, had her original tonnage of 777 lifted by the new regulations to 823.

As the most intense experiment in American ship design came in the middle of the period during which the English law was more uniformly fair than the American one, there seems to be no excuse for using tonnage restrictions as the reason why England was so much more tardy than America in producing fast ships. Both countries, up to the application of the law of 1835, were adversely affected by the old tonnage rules, but even before that the English had more incentive to make their ships narrow than the Americans had. From 1836 to 1864 the Americans alone were handicapped by a system that made full-built ships relatively cheaper per true ton to own.

The real answer, on both counts, was admitted by the British scientist and student of naval architecture, Augustin F. B. Creuze, who wrote about 1840 a ninety-page article on shipbuilding for the *Encyclopaedia Britannica's* Seventh Edition. It is the more significant and revealing because none of the famous Yankee clippers had been launched before he wrote. He was referring to American ships in general, and to the best examples he would have had a chance to examine, which were the packets of the famous Atlantic Shuttle, or Rail Road Route.

Creuze wrote, "The merchant princes of England, with their boundless wealth, proverbial generosity, and persevering enterprise, might surely have attracted the attention of men of science to the improvement of their argosies. That they have not done so is indisputable . . . the mercantile navy of England is the least speedy and most unsafe that belongs to a civilized nation."

Admitting that similar causes have operated to check the progress of both the American and British merchant fleets, he added that it was the American merchantmen which were supplanting England's, and said, "We cannot evade the conclusion, that the reason for this must be found in the inefficiency and inadequacy of the ships themselves, and that the absence of all improvement in our mercantile navy has placed it in this disadvantageous position. . . .

"Peace found America in possession of an immense commercial navy, which, on an average, could perform its passages in one-third less time than our own; and although this is necessarily attained by some sacrifice of capacity, the result has shown the sacrifice to have been judicious. The peace also found America in possession of ship-builders who had made the improvement of the qualities of ships their study. She therefore was not only in possession of a better mercantile navy, with which to compete with us, but she had also the vantage-ground of superior knowledge, and a far more extended experience, from which to start for the future competition. . . .

"England possesses upwards of two millions and a half

of tonnage in inferior shipping; and the merchant builders of Britain . . . are, with a few honorable exceptions, unequal to the task of competition with the more educated and more practiced foreigner."

Writing some while after the repeal of the stupid old tonnage law, Creuze admitted that it had taken men many years even to realize the direct influence of that law on the forms of ships, and that a generation which had been brought up in the belief that such forms were normal and right had not even begun to recover from their erroneous view.

When England did bestir herself again, upon the sea, she did it magnificently—as Americans have rueful reason to know. Our pre-eminence won in the days of the Yankee clippers slipped away while our Civil War was distracting the whole country. The next great national effort turned inland, to conquer a mere solid continent instead of a watery world. But when Creuze wrote, in the hope of rallying his own countrymen with a few words of blunt truth in England's most respected encyclopaedia, the most exciting chapter of all in the supremacy of Yankee shipbuilding had not yet opened.

CHAPTER EIGHTEEN

It has been easy, in the career of Nat Palmer, to trace most of the influences and events that pushed Americans, despite the tonnage formula, ever more urgently toward the improvement of their ships. Some day, when proper histories are written, N. B. Palmer ought to loom larger as a man more important in America and the world than most of the admirals or generals of his own time whose names are better known. From the day when he found a new continent, in an offhand fashion that makes the vast expeditions of later explorers seem a trifle silly, Nat Palmer was much in the public eye. He wrote little about himself, but others who knew him have left affectionate accounts. In the "Shipping Intelligence" columns of old newspapers we can keep track of his comings and goings throughout the period with which this book is concerned.

Nat Palmer symbolized the practice of "try it and see." Out of wide experience came hunches, and one of his hunches, when it was tried by Collins, achieved the first great step toward the ultimate clippers.

In the cases of Griffiths and McKay the records are not so helpful. Although both were somewhat opinionated, neither was so spectacular as Nat Palmer, who in personal behavior was the most reserved of the three. McKay worked methodically, building with assurance from the first. But for years he was only one of many good shipbuilders. The world took no exceptional notice of him until he was on the threshold of his tremendous achievements. He was known as a very competent shipwright, then as a very competent builder. There were no early hints in his career, as in Nat Palmer's, of what was coming. McKay wrote little about himself. He let his products tell their own story on the sea routes of history and in the memory of men.

Of Griffiths as a person we know even less than we do of McKay, but his personality appears strongly in his writing—and he wrote, for a man of his profession, a great deal. He was the son of a shipwright, and was born in New York in 1809. I can find no record of early seafaring in his case. References in his books indicate, however, that he at some time studied the behavior of ships in their own element. His father early trained him as a shipwright, but a strong faculty for mathematics and draughtsmanship soon elevated him from the yard to the mould loft and the drafting table. He worked for a while at the Gosport Navy Yard in Portsmouth, Virginia, preparing plans. He has been cred-

ited with designing, at the age of nineteen, a frigate named
the *Macedonian*, which was built to replace the one of that
name captured by Joshua Humphreys' *United States*. It is
more probable, however, that Griffiths prepared final working plans from the designs of Samuel Humphreys, Joshua's
son, who was the official naval constructor at the Gosport
Yard. Griffiths, as a matter of fact, was really twenty-three
when the frigate was laid down. In 1836 he began to contribute articles on naval architecture to the Portsmouth
Advocate. Soon afterward he returned to New York to work
as a draughtsman for the firm of Smith and Dimon.

Griffiths, like Palmer and like Pook as well, who was to
appear somewhat later on the scene with sudden brilliance,
inherited a shipbuilding tradition. But McKay was the son
of a farmer. If he did not derive from his immediate fore-
bears the rudiments of his profession, he did get the odd
Scottish temperament that has bewildered Englishmen
since before the days of the Bruce: a deceptive surface
shrewdness that masks a Celtic dream of wild glory and
sometimes lets it burst suddenly forth, as it was to do in
the early Eighteen Fifties, from a shipyard in East Boston.

Donald McKay was born beside a river named Jordan,
in Nova Scotia, on September 4th, 1810. The ripples of
Jordan Bay proved more attractive than the furrows of the
farm both to Donald and to his younger brother Lauchlan.
When as boys they built a fishing boat together, because
the family was too poor to buy one, destiny had fixed upon
both. There was a kind of harmonious understanding between the two, all their lives. It is important to remember
this circumstance, because Donald, who was very seldom
on the water himself, kept in touch with the shipmaster's

point of view through Lauchlan, who was both builder and skipper by turns.

The firths of Nova Scotia always have been littered with little shipyards. In those near Shelburne at least three of Hugh McKay's many sons early found employment. Having been schooled by shipwright neighbors in ingenuity and the rules of thumb, Donald knew at sixteen what his vocation was to be and emigrated with characteristic directness to New York, which already had a reputation for building the best large vessels belonging to America. There, after a brief interlude as a day laborer, he signed an indenture of apprenticeship to Isaac Webb "to learn the art, trade and mystery of a ship-carpenter." For the term of four years, six months, and eleven days, he agreed to work at $2.50 a week and to shun completely the perils of ale-houses, taverns, dance houses or playhouses, cards, dice, and matrimony.

In the latter Eighteen Twenties, when McKay and Griffiths were learning that art-trade-and-mystery, shipbuilding was still based almost entirely upon hand methods and inspiration. A few scientists had made careful experiments with models pulled in tanks by weights at the ends of cords fed over pulleys, but the models used, owing to a passion for scientific first principles, had generally been of a form to discourage the practical builder from taking even a cautious second look at the published treatises that resulted from these essentially most worthy efforts. The scientists and the practical men were still miles apart, and were not really to be brought together until Griffiths began to write and to lecture for the public.

Isaac Webb did not produce many remarkable ships

himself, before his partnership with Allen, but he did something more important in the long run: he produced two brilliant apprentices, his own son William and young Donald McKay. The older Webb's yard was old fashioned, but Isaac's knowledge was basic and sound. His two pupils thus had a chance to grow with the art.

This was the general procedure, in those days:

A merchant proposed the building of a ship and agreed to take perhaps four shares in her himself, at $2000 a share. He then signed up others for eleven of the remaining twelve shares. With the last one still unsold, he went to Isaac Webb, and laid his pledges on the drawing board. After a judicious amount of bargaining, it was agreed that a ship of not less than 500 tons measurement could be built for $32,000, and that Webb himself would take the sixteenth share. Before the final papers were signed, however, a model was prepared for the approval of the investors.

This, called a lift model, was made of alternate layers of wood, usually cedar and pine, the lowest layer or lift being about twice as thick as the others in Isaac Webb's heyday. Having determined the main dimensions, Webb first would sketch the midship section, or dead flat, identified on most plans of vessels by the symbol $\oplus$. The midship section was defined as the one which, at right angles to the water line, would be the largest in area. To put it another way, it was a plane cutting through the fattest part of the vessel. The method of deciding the shape of the dead flat deserves some attention by itself, a little later, because it illustrates so well the rule-of-thumb fallacies that survived well past Isaac Webb's days in the great navies of the world. Probably, in most such cases, the dead flat of the last ship designed for a similar trade was examined, and was altered a bit in the new plan, mainly by hunch, on a supposed basis of the reports of the former vessel's performance at sea.

The dead flat was bisected by a vertical line. The lifts, held together snugly by dowels, were set up with one side planed smooth, and the plan of half the dead flat was traced on each end. The model then was planed down to a solid form having the contour of the dead flat throughout its whole length. After that, it was up to the shipbuilder's eye. He would file and whittle the lift model to the form which, in his judgment, seemed best to carry forward and aft the arbitrary lines of the dead flat.

As a rule, the part of the original form left untouched in the whittling, the fattest section representing the true dead flat in the finished model, was located either $\frac{2}{5}$ths or $\frac{1}{3}$ of the way from the stem or forward end. The lowest lift had been made thick to take care of the fact that a properly designed ship in the Eighteen Twenties always had an after drag: was shallower forward. The logic behind this was the same as that which caused the first ancient seaman to tip his square sail upward to make a lateen, and catch the wind on a "leading edge" slanting firmly all the way, instead of on the shorter luff of the loose canvas itself. The long keel, gradually deepening as it proceeded aft, was just such a leading edge upside down. It supposedly provided a better grip on the water all the way fore and aft, keeping the ship steady.

When the model was approved, it was taken apart and a series of parallel lines were drawn on paper, representing the planes where the upper and lower edges of the separate lifts came into contact. The vertical frames then were drawn, beginning with the dead flat and proceeding both

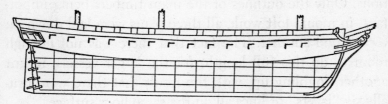

ways. The general outline could be sketched in by laying the lifts edgewise on their corresponding locations on the plan itself. The first result was called the sheer plan.

Next the half-breadth plan was made, by tracing around the individual lifts one at a time, and by continuing from

the sheer plan the vertical lines which indicated the locations of the frames. Finally the body plan was prepared. This could be done from the other two plans, beginning with the original dead flat and filling in the contours of the other frames by measurement from the first two drawings.

The next step was to lay the lines down full size on the floor of the mould loft. This was one of the chief aspects of the "mystery" of ship-carpentry. The lofts in early days had been big enough for full-size drawings of entire ships. Or, to put it the other way, the ships had been small enough to be drawn full size in the average loft. As the size of ships increased it became necessary to draw them in sections. Only the outlines of the main timbers being important, in mould loft work, all three plans were laid down on top of one another. The fact that there was not enough room to do this full length, for the larger vessels, meant another doubling up, with the result that there were usually six "layers" of lines all on the same floor surface.

A stranger, coming into the loft at that point and looking at the pattern of weaving, crisscrossing curves, well might have agreed that the apprentices, young Webb and the newcomer from Nova Scotia, were being taught a "mystery." In practice it was not quite so jumbled as it sounds, or as it looked either. Different colors of chalk were used on the black-painted floor to distinguish the different plans. The practiced eye could pick one plan out by the color, ignoring the others.

The plans on paper had been made to scale, usually 1/4 inch representing one foot of the final ship. In transferring the plan to the floor, a special ruler was used, marked to read 48 times the true distance on the drawing. If two points on the plan really were 4 1/4 inches apart, the special ruler laid between them would indicate it as 17 feet. Then a long batten stick, marked in feet and inches, was laid on the floor to mark the corresponding distance and a nail was driven at the proper point. Along a series of such nails, flexible battens were bent to follow the curve, and the final line chalked along the curving batten strip.

When the plans were all laid down on the floor, the moulds were prepared. There were several kinds of moulds. Some were cut like dressmakers' patterns from thin wood to

MOULD-LOFTING

show the precise curvature of the timbers, full size. Others were merely straight pieces laid on the floor and marked with lines crossing at an angle wherever they themselves covered such a line on the floor. One mould, for example, would be used in setting up the final timbers to show the angle at which each frame should be fastened into the keel. This would appear clearly from the body plan as it was laid down on the floor.

A single mould, laid vertically at one-fourth the extreme breadth out from the keel, would be marked to show where each framing line of the plan crossed it. Later, when the ship was being framed in the yard, the same mould would be stood up successively on the ways to adjust the corresponding frame to the proper position. In this way one mould with many markings would do for a large number of operations. And once a set of moulds had been made, another ship could be built to the same dimensions without using the mould loft at all. This was not often done, but some of the moulds of a former vessel frequently could be employed in a new one, with suitable changes.

Next the timbers were selected, using the moulds to aid in choosing pieces with the best natural curvature. Adzmen dubbed one surface of each timber to an approximate plane, turned it over, and did a more precise job on the other surface. The timber then was placed across a saw pit, and with the aid of the mould was chalked to shape. One sawyer, following the chalk line, stood on the timber itself. The other, wearing a cap with netting to keep the sawdust out of his eyes, held the other end of the saw down in the pit.

Blocks were laid for the keel down an incline called the

groundways which led into the water. The slope usually was one inch to the foot, or a little less. Then began the intricate process of assembling the heavy pieces of the frame. These, in Isaac Webb's time, were all heaved into place on the shoulders of the workmen, although the heavier single timbers sometimes weighed as much as a ton. The backbone of the ship, which was the keel with its stem and sternpost, was made of many large, separate pieces "fayed" together with intricately cut joints to add to the strength of the whole structure. These joints always were bolted, but bolts in those days were not threaded, nor were they fastened with nuts. They were straight rods, one end of which had been forged to a head, like big, pointless nails. The bolts were driven through holes not quite large enough to have received them by less lusty persuasions. A kind of washer then was dropped over the protruding plain end, which was hammered like a rivet until the end of the rod mushroomed out over the ring. That was why the phrase, in reference to repairs, always was "drawing" a bolt. It had to be gripped at one end with a special tool and literally torn out of the wood, unless one end could first be got at with a cold chisel and cut off. Then the bolt might be driven out.

Most of the fastening, in old ships, was done with tree-nails: wooden pins pounded into auger holes and clinched on the inside of the vessel by splitting the ends and driving a little wedge into them. When the main pieces of the frame all had been erected, adjusted in accordance with their moulds, and held by temporary ribbands and harpins, the planking and ceiling were put on with treenails. Ceiling, it may be well to explain, referred in a ship to something more underfoot than overhead. It was the layer of planking inside the ribs or frames of the vessel.

The intricate processes of shipbuilding, if they were all to be traced and illustrated, would require a full book and a fat one. Even before the scientific method produced sound laws to replace notions about the shape of ships, their construction called for much mathematical skill and precision. Norie's revised manual of shipbuilding, published at about the time when Griffiths and McKay were receiving their early training, devoted its first 79 pages to problems in general mathematics, geometry, trigonometry, and the use of a special slide rule manufactured for shipwrights. Many small craft were turned out more by luck and guesswork than by science, and some of them were not bad. But such a builder as Isaac Webb had used his rule, his table of densities, and his technical knowledge of hydrostatics to such a degree that the load waterline marked on his draft before building began, would be the line on the finished product to which the water would rise when she was laded to her true (not her measurement) tonnage.

The appearance of Norie's manual in an inexpensive edition was a sign of the times. The earlier treatises had either been incomplete or exceedingly expensive because of the many large plates thought indispensable. The firm of Norie produced a work, as they phrased it, "compatible with the resources of the professional class, for which it is more peculiarly intended." The common laborer was winning his right to an education, through books. Poor boys, shipwrights' and farmers' sons, were about to take over the theory of shipbuilding and to shape it anew, far better than it had been shaped before their time by the more highly privileged naval architects.

British naval architecture, as a matter of fact, always had fared better at the hands of humble and practical men. The treatises of Mungo Murray, a "mechanic," had been more widely read in England during the Eighteen Hundreds than the works of noblemen who were given technical charge of the design of King's ships. But the noblemen lacked practice and the practical men, although sometimes fine mathematicians like Murray, lacked a real insight into the branch of physics called hydrostatics. Creuze, in his famous Britannica article, complained that the class prejudices of England had prevented such men as Murray from advancing to the eminence and influence they might have attained.

But in the New World, such youngsters as John Griffiths and Donald McKay could acquire both the great dream of the perfect ship and a necessary practical competence to make it come true.

CHAPTER NINETEEN

DONALD MC KAY AND JOHN GRIFFITHS, AIDING IN THE building of ships out of thousands of pieces intricately fitted by hand, had to acquire, if they were to excel, a knowledge of mathematics by no means trifling in comparison with that of the engineer of today. But the mechanical procedures of a century and a quarter ago were still primitive. There were as yet no machine tools in the shipyards. The quantity manufacture of even carpenters' hand tools had scarcely begun. New York's first true "hardware stores" were innovations when McKay arrived in 1826. Ironmongers still were making most of the tools on individual order, and delivering them with the cutting edges rough-hammered—tempered but unground.

It would be morally instructive to discover that Donald, and his brother Lauchlan who soon followed him, triumphed by sheer grit over all sorts of difficulties. But their brand of genius—both shared it—seems not to have been endangered by considerate treatment. Donald soon was asking to be released from his indenture, perhaps because of the clause prohibiting marriage. When Mr Webb kindly granted the young man's wish, Donald soon married a shipbuilder's daughter who brought with her a nest egg big enough to allow the young couple to live in comfort.

On his own in the early Eighteen Thirties, Donald worked at several of the East River yards, gathering with a Scottish thoroughness all the available knowledge of new methods as fast as they were adopted by the most enterprising set of builders on earth. He saw the first derricks erected, operated by steam power, and the first engine-driven saws for cutting timber. Treenails, which formerly had been "drifted" out of oak and locust blocks with a hatchet, purposely made octagonal with the idea that it gave them a better grip, began to come from lathes, more rapidly and turned to a precise diameter. In a way this was a pity. Some of the masterly old skill of the shipwrights degenerated when machines came in. Carpenters had been proud of their skill in rapidly splitting out "trunnels" that could be little improved for accuracy by measurement and careful planing. Some of them, using only an adz, could hew out a rectangular keel timber, taking a clean whole chip every time, and ending with a surface having so slight a ripple that further finishing was unnecessary.

They were quick and precise. The machine-saw was quicker and a little more precise, and so the old skill of

the artisan disappeared. But as perfection in handicraft lessened, the ideal of perfection in the form of a ship grew.
Donald McKay may have worked on the *Garrick, Sheridan,
Siddons,* or *Roscius.* Perhaps he worked on more than one
of them, for it is known that he was employed by their
builders, Brown & Bell, during the years of their construction from 1836 to 1838. They proved for a time, by performance, what the dead flat of a fast and capacious ship
should look like.

The dream of the perfect ship seems always to have
grown from the dead flat, or midships section, because that
was the way the draftsman proceeded. Perhaps we should
jog back a bit, to see how the mathematical dream first
shaped up. It is tempting to believe that the Arabs, great
mathematicians and scientists of a thousand or fifteen hundred years ago, scientifically evolved the forms of the ships
that carried them on their eastward conquests. But I have
seen no evidence to establish it as a fact.

Very good midship sections were evolved by Norsemen,
as the petrified remains of one or two Viking vessels attest.
Here too we have no proof that the form resulted from any
process more theoretical than the old "try-it-and-see." The
French mathematician Fournier, early in the Sixteen Hundreds, approached the problem with some effort at the scientific method by assuming that a circle, which contains
the greatest possible area within the shortest possible
boundary line, was the ideal midship section with which to
begin, because it would hold the greatest amount of cargo
while it presented the least surface to the friction of the
water.

Such a circle, uniformly loaded, would roll uncontrollably, and be unable to sustain a mast or sail. Therefore, Fournier reasoned, it should be given an even keel to float on by chopping off a part of the bottom of the circle. This, he thought, should also be shaped from arcs of a circle.

Fournier's theoretical dead flat happened to be very similar to the form in use in the French navy at the time. It is hard to avoid the suspicion that he altered his first ideal circle in such a way as to justify what was known to work anyhow. He did not explain upon what basis of sound physical law he chopped off just so much, and no more, of the bottom of the circle, or just why he used more arcs to do it. If he had stuck to his original contention that one of the two basic conditions was maximum content for the dead flat, he would have bent the shorter arcs the other way, or at least would have used straight lines. But he assumed that the surface must be a series of curves, and that the amount of the curvature should be determined by the principle that the two arcs should melt into each other without forming an "arc angle." Why he assumed the necessity of using only arcs of true circles he never explained, except for the idea of the original circle.

Dead flats produced by Fournier's rule and by Bouguer, who modified it a hundred years later, were commonly used well into the Eighteen Hundreds. Although their use began so much earlier, they represented a kind of bad compromise between the fast-sailing, sharp-floored vessels typical of the American blockade runners, and the fast-sailing, flat-floored packets of a later date. Unfortunately, they put the virtues of each type in the wrong place, and got the full advantage of neither. Fournier's dead flat had a flattish floor right at the edges of the keel, but it did not extend

far enough out to be very useful. The quicker curve upward, above that, sacrificed cargo space and steadiness
without achieving any of the virtues of a sharp dead rise
beginning at the keel.

Another Frenchman named De Palmi proposed a somewhat more complicated mathematical method of construct-
ing the dead flat of a vessel with flatter floors, and Bouguer
evolved similar rules for making a sharper one. It is unnecessary to explain the complications of procedure in
either case, so long as notice is taken of the fact that all of
these assume that the section should be made up of arcs of
circles. The process had started with a sensible geometrical
idea: to get the greatest content with the least surface.
After that, they went on using arcs of a circle for no reason
at all. On the other hand, it was obvious to the rule-of-
thumb builders that if a vessel was to be prevented from
rolling back and forth—they would have said, if she was to
be made stiff rather than crank—then sharp corners might
be more useful than curves.

These practical designers gave to the early Baltimore
clipper schooners, and to other fast-sailing types evolved
in the blockade-running days, a sharp V-bottom amidships
gradually curving up in an arc that did not pretend to be
part of a true circle. And the Baltimore schooners ran away
from the frigates built according to Bouguer, whereas they
in turn had no trouble in catching up with the merchantmen designed by De Palmi and his disciples. Later, Nat
Palmer gave the packets a flat floor with comparatively
sharp outer "corners" and a nearly straight line upward
from there.

Even though a square form was technically not so capacious as a round one having the same perimeter, Nat Palmer's type of dead flat, with the same beam for tonnage measurement as that of a De Palmi ship, stowed more goods in those extra corners, and the corners reduced the tendency to be crank.

It was thus, in the days of Griffiths' and McKay's apprenticeship and early professional labors, that practical experience freed naval architecture from a kind of narrow, pure science that left the realities out of account. It had been a science working scrupulously and with great accuracy from principles that never had been proved in the first place, and which happened to be wrong. There was only a hunch, and an incorrect one, behind the idea that a midship section must be built up of true arcs of circles. When that erroneous rubbish of ideas was cleared away, the central part of the dream of the perfect ship was back where it had been in the great days of the Vikings, and practical scientists like Griffiths could start anew.

Griffiths himself early realized that the argument over sharp versus flat floor was only part of the problem, and that the effect of the tonnage laws also was confusing. The factor of tax-free depth had worked most to the relative disadvantage of the English. Their ships presently became so deep as to be unsafe and unsteady. Creuze thought that many ships had capsized because of this feature alone.

Griffiths began by clearing the tonnage laws out of his mind altogether. He had the advantage of working in the Navy Yard for a time, where the tonnage rules had no effect because naval ships were not taxed. Thus he was able to think things out again from the beginning. His first contribution had to do with longitudinal shape.

I have tried to give a brief indication of the mathematical idea of the dead flat, and its development, up to Griffiths' day. The carrying of that outline forward and backward to bow and stern was based sometimes upon mathematical ideas of a very advanced and complicated sort, sometimes upon common sense and experience. Most popular of all was a third method, called "Whole Moulding," accomplished with the aid of two moulds curving in opposite directions. These were cut in the first place to the same shape as the curvature of the dead flat. Then, in drawing the frames fore and aft on the mould loft floor, the upper mould was moved inward a certain indicated amount for each new frame, and the lower mould moved up against it to maintain contact. But this procedure too was not based on any sure knowledge as to why these two curves, moving against each other, always would produce exactly the right shape for each frame.

Mathematicians also worked out complicated formulas which, when applied by the draftsman, would produce a "rising line" and other arbitrary lines on the plan in such a way that a ship would result, looking more or less like the ones built by common sense and experience, but still not proved to be a good shape for any particular and clear reason.

CHAPTER TWENTY

THE PRACTICAL BUILDER, ALL ALONG, DID THE PRACTICAL thing. He looked at natural objects that lived in the water and on it: at fish and waterfowl. The typical ship built without the aid of fancy theories was designed, as closely as the tonnage laws would permit, like that part of a duck which is observable from under water. The practical builders who worked directly from nature argued that a waterfowl was a better model than a fish because it, like a ship, would have been designed to operate partly out of water and in the wind.

Nevertheless, the favorite expression based on nature was, "A codfish head and a mackerel tail." Isaac Newton, in the latter Sixteen Hundreds, had evolved by mathemaical study a form which he called *the solid of least resistance*. It was undoubtedly in the minds of mathematical scientists when they designed the half-breadth plan of a ship. The dimensions Newton gave his solid, length three times the breadth, persisted as the ideal dimensions for ships too.

Practical men had yet another expression concerning the form of the perfect ship. They said, "It makes no difference how roughly you push the water apart with the bows so long as you bring it together cleanly again with the stern." Suction caused by turbulent water under the stern, according to their theory, dragged back on the ship with a force greater than that presented against the bows by water that was undisturbed.

John Griffiths saw the plain fallacy in that argument. He realized that bows and sterns were two separate problems. To him it made no sense to declare, as the saying did, that if you solved one of the two problems you could forget about the other one. Unquestionably, the turbulence under the stern of a vessel acted as a drag. But John Griffiths wondered whether a large part of that turbulence might not be caused by roughly disturbing the water with blunt bows. He settled down to read everything he could find on the subject. In the course of his reading he came upon an enormous book entitled—*Nautical and Hydraulic Experiments, with numerous scientific miscellanies*. By Colonel Mark Beaufoy, F.R.S. &c.

Beaufoy's work was published in 1834, when Griffiths was twenty-five. It is an indication of the British shipbuilders' indifference to scientific efforts on their behalf that the experiments which the book recorded had been finished more than thirty-five years earlier. Beaufoy had reported the results to learned societies, but the world at large did not get an adequate knowledge of his work until after his death.

Mark Beaufoy was the son of a prosperous English brewer. When he was fourteen years old he heard "an eminent mathematician" say that if a cone were pulled through the water blunt end first it would offer less resistance than if it were pulled sharp end foremost. Young Mark had the common sense not to believe it. What was more important, he decided to try it and see. He immediately had a cone made by a local turner, rigged up a pulley on the edge of a vat in the brew house, tied a heavy bunch of keys to one end of a cord with the cone fastened to the other end—and tried it—and saw.

He discovered that the same bunch of keys pulled the cone more slowly blunt end first than sharp end foremost. After that he made a great many experiments with this apparatus, but later rigged up a better one in which a long heavy pendulum provided the motive power. By fastening differently shaped objects to the bottom of the pendulum, so that the objects to be tested would be immersed but the pendulum would not, he had a means of comparing different shapes, to see by trying it which offered least resistance to the water. When pulled to a specified distance in one direction, and then allowed to swing free with nothing attached, the pendulum always reached a fixed point on the end of the scale before it stopped and reversed. The greater the resistance of the immersed object attached to it, the shorter would be the stroke. By reading the scale and finding the exact distance of the swing for each separate form, it was easy to tell which had least resistance. The free pendulum, with nothing attached, would swing 27.85 inches, as set up for the first series of experiments. When a piece of wood shaped to the specifications of Newton's solid of least resistance was attached, the swing was very nearly as great: 27.00 inches. A cylinder "with a semi-ellipsis joined to one end" swung 25.95 inches. Half a sphere swung 24.00 inches with the rounded side foremost, and 15.50 inches when turned the other way. That was the worst reading from any of the many forms that were tried.

In the early series of trials two objects proved to have even less resistance than Newton's "ideal" solid. One of them is described as a "circular spindle whose fore part was two inches and whose after part was 4 inches; in other words, it was ⅓ longer than the other solids." As all of the objects had the same thickness at the middle, this one, in swinging 27.10 inches, seemed to prove that greater length reduced the resistance of the water, even though the total area of wood and water in contact was greater and could be expected to cause greater friction.

The other object which improved on Newton is described in such a way that I cannot confidently decide what it really did look like. Here, for what it is worth, is Beaufoy's own hasty laboratory note: "Sir Isaac Newton's solid of least resistance, with the middle made triangular, or rather it was a circular spindle, there being no sensible difference between one solid and the other on so small a scale."

Two of Beaufoy's early conclusions are notable: 1. "—increasing the length of a solid, of almost any form, by the addition of a cylinder in the middle, exceedingly diminishes the resistance with which it moves, provided the weight in water continue to be the same. A fact, I apprehend, that cannot be easily explained." 2. "—the Experiments clearly prove that a ship will move through the water with the least resistance when her greatest breadth is distant from the bow two-fifths of her whole length."

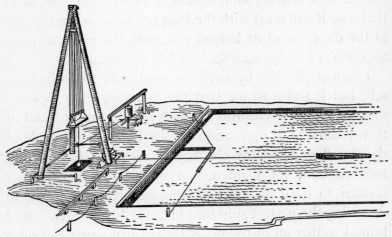

In connection with the latter remark, Beaufoy refers to "The common opinion, that the greatest breadth of a ship should be given to the middle." This is hard to understand, because an examination of plans of ships built at the time when he wrote, or earlier, shows the greatest breadth typically at a distance of ⅖ths from the bow, as he recommends. Breadth in the larger ships was almost the same from a point slightly aft of amidships to a point ¼th of the ship's length from the bow. But the exact widest point, by a very narrow margin, was always forward of amidships in all plans I have seen.

Beaufoy's final experiments were made with very large

models drawn along the surface of an outdoor pool by great weights that first were hoisted high in the air by a windlass with a horse providing the power.

Griffiths conducted tank experiments of his own, probably checking up on Beaufoy. With this in mind it is interesting to observe yet another of Beaufoy's findings: "The bottom of a floating solid should be made triangular, as in that case it will meet with the least resistance when moving in the direction of its longest axis, with the greatest resistance when moving with its broadside foremost."

I cannot prove it by anything written by Griffiths himself, but it seems to me that this sentence from Beaufoy may have started Griffiths off on a line of thought and of theory directly in opposition to Nat Palmer's principle of the flat floor. Griffiths checked everything painstakingly, took nothing for granted, not even what Nat Palmer seemed to have proved. But the great thing he did, in dreaming the perfect ship into life, was to co-ordinate and bring together all of the many factors that worked at once to aid or retard the final purpose. His mind was the first, in the history of naval architecture, that could comprehend all at the same time the intricate changing interplay of many forces, from both wind and water, affecting the final shape.

All tank experiments such as Beaufoy's had concerned themselves only with head-on resistance of water to a force pushing in one direction, with the object held steadily in one position. But a ship, as Griffiths knew, got its force from any one of twenty of the compass card's thirty-two points, excluding only the six points on each side of the bowsprit. The force always tipped the form somewhat, perhaps very far indeed. Moreover, the force, although it was resolved at a single point, was applied at three points, in a ship, where the centers of three different masts intersected the line of lateral resistance, below decks. Thus the center of effort would shift with alterations in the wind or in the distribution of sails.

The problem, Griffiths concluded, was to reduce the head-on resistance as much as possible, and at the same time to increase the helpful, leeway resistance presented—not merely broadside-on as Beaufoy had written—but at any point forward of the beam from which the wind might be blowing. This must be done, also, in such a way that this sidewise resistance would increase more and more, the greater the force of the wind, heeling the ship over from an upright position.

Finally, and perhaps most important of all, the form must be further refined to take care of the change in its own resistance, the shift in its own line of flotation, caused by the extra speed produced in these ways.

```
╭══════════════════════════════════════╮
║                                        ║
║          CHAPTER TWENTY-ONE            ║
║                                        ║
╰══════════════════════════════════════╯
```

H AVE YOU EVER NOTICED, IN A MOTOR-DRIVEN SPEED-
boat, how the bows tend to rise more and more as the
speed increases? What is equally important to the designer
of a hull, the stern also sinks in the trough formed by the
water-splitting action of the bows. In the smallest kind of
powered craft, with an outboard motor, the propeller seems
to be pulling the stern downward. So it does, by hauling
the water out from under it. But a similar vessel, given
velocity by other means, will do somewhat the same thing.

Try it and see. Saw off an 18-inch piece of two by four,
with a couple of 45° cuts to form the bows. Give it a push
in still water. Better still, have someone else push it while
you crouch with your eyes near water level. You will see

that the forward end rises and the after end sinks. This is true even when the bows are cut straight up and down, with no flare to help them coast up above the surface. The greater the speed, the more obviously the forward end rises and the after end sinks.

At really high speeds, an unweighted object of this kind will "plane" up on the surface. Then it becomes a different kind of vessel—a hydroplane—with problems of its own. Merchant ships have different problems for our attention. They operate with the larger part of their hulls immersed. The behavior of that part of the hull which may be under water in any kind of weather is the chief concern of the naval architect.

It was this problem—behavior with *increase* of speed—that fascinated John Griffiths. I remember no hint, in the writings of his predecessors, that the *rate* of travel was considered important in shaping a hull. Yet the simple experiment just outlined indicates that the shape of the hull itself really changes as the speed increases. From the considerations of hydrostatics, the only part of the hull which matters is the part below waterline. When speed causes the bows to rise out of water and the stern to sink deeper, the shape of the hull itself is changed. Its bows become shallower, and its after drag increases.

This fact gave Griffiths his most important clue toward improvement of the forms of ships. There was scant hope of increasing the maximum speed if ships continued to be built in such a way that, the faster they went, the more their bottoms would tilt to press against the water. Up to the time of the first English blockades of America, no ships were designed with a hope of sailing faster than ten or twelve knots. Logs of supposedly fast fighting craft of the Revolutionary period seldom show an entry of more than eight knots. Inside that speed, the change in the line of flotation was not very noticeable for heavily laden ships. A foremast set far forward, and sometimes square sails out on the sprit, applied a strong leverage to press the bows down with an increase of wind. By this magnificently muddle-headed device, the possibility of real speed was eliminated. In order that the ship might not tilt upward, "dragging her tail" deep in the water and thus slowing her speed, a leverage was provided which slowed her speed anyhow by pushing the blunt, resistant bows more firmly down.

There had been ships with sharp bows, under water, long before Griffiths' day, but Griffiths appears to have been the first to regard the problem of bow design with the definite purpose of keeping the "trim" of the vessel constant at all speeds. Instead of pressing the bows down by sail leverage, he realized that the thing to do was to cut them to a shape which would have a minimum tendency to rise in the first place.

Griffiths worked out his theories on the drafting board and in the model tank about the year 1840, but was unsuccessful in convincing anyone of their practicality. Each year, in those days, an exhibition was held, by an organization known as the American Institute of the City of New York, to call new inventions to the notice of the business community. At the Institute's fair of 1842 Griffiths showed a model embodying his ideas. Seven years later he wrote, "It was not, however, well received at that time, but has since been regarded as an improvement, and adopted as such."

This model has been the subject of a great deal of careless writing by enthusiasts. It is usually referred to as the first one having "hollow bows" or at least "hollow water lines." Griffiths himself, so far as I can discover in his writings, never made this claim. So scrupulous a student must have known at least of the plans of earlier vessels with concavities forward, *under* water. In making the reference which I have quoted above, from page 102 of his *Treatise on Marine and Naval Architecture,* he was concluding a passage that argued for a hollow flaring of the bows outward *above* the water line. He argued for bows formed in such a fashion, both above and below the normal water line, that their downward resistance would be increased very sharply if they should tend to bury, whereas both downward and head-on resistance would be at a practical minimum when the ship was floating on an even keel. The main argument of the older designers for codfish bows was the need for buoyancy when the ship pitched. Because they did not want to risk the possibility of seeing her head plunge under a wave, they made her buoyant and full-bowed for all conditions. In using foresight against troubles that might be met with when her line of flotation was violently disturbed, once in a while, they made her slow and logy all of the time.

Griffiths, on the other hand, so formed his bows that the fullness would be well above water in all normal circumstances, and would come into play to retard the burying of the ship's head only when the tendency to bury actually did occur: when she plunged downward, into a rising wave. Specifically, at the point in his text where he mentions his

American Institute model he is arguing for a concave cut-water, or stem.

Before Griffiths revolutionized the art, it was the custom of ship designers to carry the "rabbet" (the line where the actual planking terminated in a groove chiseled into the heavy timber of the sternpost, keel, and stem) upward in a convex or apple-cheeked curve. A quick look at older ships may give the impression that the bows are concave, but really it is only the relatively flat timber called the cutwater that curves outward as it rises. The line of the planking, the true body of the ship, curled farther toward the vertical as it came up above water.

Let us look in succession at the bows of three ships: a merchantman of the Eighteenth Century; Humphrey's fastest frigate, the *Philadelphia;* and a typical Griffiths clipper. Each of the curving lines on the right-hand section of the body plan represents a cross section. The second line from the left on the top plan, the first curving line—again from the left—on the middle plan, and the third curve from the left on the bottom plan all represent cross sections at about equivalent locations through the bows of the three ships. Note first that the bows of the Indiaman were built as if to bounce on the waves like a ball.

It is now easy to see what Griffiths wanted. The *Philadelphia,* about as speedy as an ordnance carrier modeled in the old fashion could be, had rather sharp bows under water. Her dead flat was located ⅖ths of the distance from the stem. But in the vertical cross section chosen for comparison, cutting through the point at which the stem fays into the keel, her bows were already curving toward the vertical as they rose above normal waterline. From there on

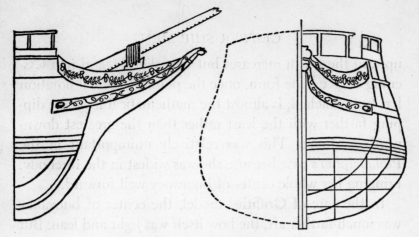

AN EAST INDIAMAN, ABOUT 1760

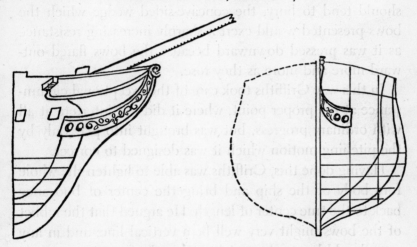

THE "PHILADELPHIA," LAUNCHED 1799

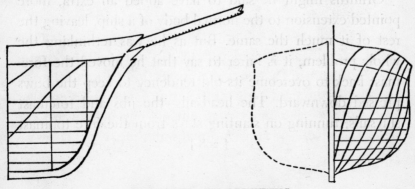

A CLIPPER, BY GRIFFITHS

upward the width increases but very slightly, and in a lessening degree. The form, once the point of normal flotation has been reached, is almost the mathematical ideal for dipping farther with the least rather than the greatest downward resistance. This was relatively unimportant in the *Philadelphia's* case because she was widest in the forebody, bringing her whole center of buoyancy well forward.

In the case of Griffiths' model, the center of buoyancy was much farther aft, the bow itself was light and lean. But a glance at the comparative lines will show that if the head should tend to bury, the concave-sided wedge which the bows presented would exert a sharply increasing resistance as it was pressed downward because the bows flared outward more and more as they rose.

In this way Griffiths took care of the exceptional circumstance at the proper point, where it did not interfere at all with ordinary progress, but was brought into play only by the pitching motion which it was designed to correct.

Having done this, Griffiths was able to lighten the whole fore body of the ship and bring the center of buoyancy back to the true center of length. He argued that the rabbet of the bows might very well be a vertical line, and in any case should be nearly straight rather than a curve.

Griffiths might be said to have added an extra, more pointed extension to the normal body of a ship, leaving the rest of it much the same. But as he was rethinking the whole problem, it is fairer to say that he moved the foremast back to overcome its old tendency to keep the bows pressed downward. The headsails—the jibs and foremast staysails, running on slanting stays from the fore topmast and fore topgallant mast—were thus stretched at a sharper angle and tended to lift the bows more than ever.

There is a legend that the sight of Griffiths' first actual sharp ship on the stocks caused old wiseacres to predict that she would slice her way straight under the first big wave and never come up again. Her designer replied that he had removed the dangers of pitching *downward* when he moulded a hull that would not pitch *upward* in the first place with anything like the old customary violence. The traditional apple-cheeked bows were lifted high by each rising wave because they were too buoyant. Naturally the ship would slide down with a terrific plunge and splash into the next wave. Griffiths bows cut through that first wave, shedding it cleanly right and left by the flare outward above normal water line. The much lessened plunge into the next rising wave was checked without strain by an increasing wedge that had its maximum effect at the end of the downward movement rather than at the beginning. It "put on the brakes" slowly, with pressure steadily increasing to a maximum, instead of slamming them on with a jerk, which was what the old, too buoyant bow did.

Although I have been trying to explain Griffiths' treatment of the bows all by itself, his improvements did not come piecemeal. His most brilliant contribution always was his ability to conceive of the shape of his ideal ship as a whole, at all possible speeds and in all possible positions. The same reasons which made him decide to alter the shape of the bows also called for compensating changes astern. The after-drag already had been eliminated by Nat Palmer, and few ships built in the more progressive American ports after 1840 were deeper aft than they were forward. But the theory of the "fine run aft" persisted. The stretch between the fat midsection of a ship and the thin sternpost had usually been made hollow when speed was desired. So long as the center of buoyancy was kept well forward of amidships, this made little difference to the trim of the ship. Buoyancy was not needed astern. The counters and the deck above them amounted to nothing much more than a hollow platform over the rudder. This platform was built more lightly than the rest of the vessel, was known to be more subject to damage, and was balanced off in a measure by the weight of the massive bowsprit, the jibboom, and the exceptionally heavy timbers of the head.

Griffiths, after his observation of the wake of ships in the water, was convinced that the scooped-out concavity under each side of the stern was harmful from considerations of speed—and everyone knew that such lines lessened the ship's carrying capacity. Tank experiments proved to Griffiths that when any object had a depression scooped in its after part, the water swirled and bubbled in it, the agitation of the fluid acting as a drag. Accordingly, he brought the fullness of the body much farther aft than had been customary. He balanced off his sharper bow with a blunter stern. That, to the wiseacres, seemed the final folly. They were said to have chuckled over the model exhibited at the American Institute fair, saying that it would do very well if the rudder were changed to the other end and it were sailed backward. But with so much buoyancy aft, and so little forward, it seemed certain that such a ship would ram her head under and be lost.

None of them, obviously, had ever tried the simple tank experiment with a piece of two by four, to indicate the tendency of a floating body to rise forward and settle aft. Griffiths was designing ships in terms of greater speed. He knew that if he were ever to get beyond the known maximum of 13½ knots he must have finer bows that would not ride up out of the water, and a more buoyant stern that would not settle down into it too far with increasing speed.

Finally, in the complex picture he had in mind, came the effect of motive power. This, to be got from wind coming from a variety of directions, called for a longitudinal shape that would present a maximum sidewise resistance as well as a minimum resistance head-on. In the light of everything he knew and had tried, Griffiths decided that Nat Palmer's flat floor was good mainly because it carried aft in a logical fashion the fullness of bows that still were much too blunt compared with his concept. But he feared that a flat-floored vessel would be pressed to leeward too readily if the wind were abeam or ahead. Accordingly he reverted to the sharp floor, the V-bottom of early fast-sailing design.

For a year after the fair, the new model went begging. But all the factors that made for speed mania were on the increase. The China tea business was suddenly booming. China had not wanted foreign goods and foreign ideas, and for years had restricted trade to a single port. The British Government, seeking a market for the opium grown in India, fought a war with a more enlightened Chinese Government that was trying to keep the disastrous opium out. Britain's victory in 1842 (the year of Griffiths' entry in the fair of the American Institute) forced China to open several new ports to trade. American ships at once swooped to take advantage of the fact.

The China trade promptly became so rich that even a

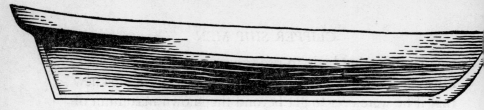

The beginnings of the clipper mould: Long, deep hollows scooped under the stern, a sharp V-bottom, greater depth aft than forward, and a rather sharp but not hollow entrance at the bows. Early Eighteen Thirties.

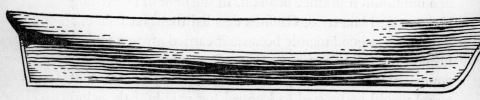

The clipper mould as developed by Griffiths: Hollows under the stern much reduced. Pronounced hollows forward, above as well as below water. Fairly sharp bottom, but the fullness of the midship section carried farther aft.

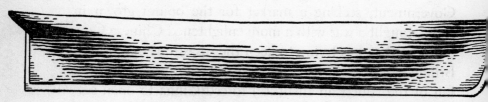

The ultimate Pook-McKay development. Flatter floor, still longer mid-section, hollow forward, slightly hollow aft.

few of the famous packet masters were lured by it, away from their already extremely well-paying profession. Commercial houses, especially in New York, realized that the vast new business of the new ports would be monopolized by the swiftest. If speed made a difference on the Atlantic run, it was even more important when running around the world and back with the main cargo so perishable a commodity as tea. News of the conclusion of the opium war brought an immediate scramble for fast ships and supermen to sail them. Nat Palmer and Bully Waterman were lured into the new trade immediately. In the *Natchez*, sister ship of the vessel which had given Palmer his experience of the fast-sailing virtues of the flat floor, Waterman came roaring home from Canton in the spring of 1843 in only 92 days, almost a record despite an eleven-year-old ship. Palmer, in the Medford-built *Paul Jones*, 624 tons, missed the favorable monsoon that year and spent weeks clawing his way down the China Sea. But when he picked up the southeast trade winds, he flew the rest of the way. His time from Anjier, in Sunda Strait between Sumatra and Java, was 79 days. That, in terms of actual distance, was about seven-eighths of the journey.

The Rail Road Route to Europe still was booming. Its ships were not easily diverted from a steadily profitable venture to a new one that might not last. The only answer was to build new ships. Howland and Aspinwall, a shrewd and close-fisted pair of partners who seldom had taken any chances, were so impressed by the boom of 1843 that in an impulsive moment they did what no-one had done before: they took John Griffiths seriously and commissioned him to build a ship for them according to his new theories.

Second thoughts came later, and in abundance. Criticism of the vessel as it shaped up on the stocks so discouraged the owners that they stopped work on her more than once. But other ships were being launched for the China trade—and they, although not so extreme as Griffiths' in design, showed a trend in the same general direction. Finally the owners threw what they may have considered to be good money after bad, and the clipper ship *Rainbow* was launched from the yard of Smith & Dimon on Washington's birthday, 1845.

The always heretical New York *Herald,* announcing the coming launch, wrote, "The *Rainbow* holds out a promise, we should judge by her model, of great speed."

The promise was fulfilled when, on the 19th of the following September, Captain John Land brought her back into the port of New York from China after a voyage of 7 months 17 days. The elapsed time included all detentions, as well as the discharging and loading of cargo. Although neither leg of the voyage set a new mark by itself, it was the fastest round voyage to China and home on record.

In the first ship in which he had been given a fair chance to do so, John Willis Griffiths had gone a long way toward proving his theories.

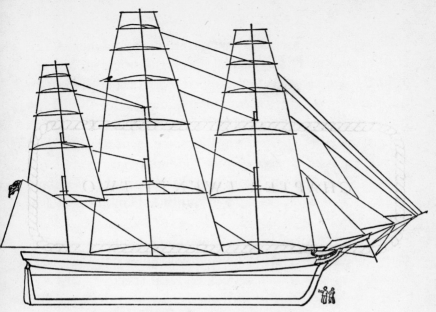

THE "RAINBOW": SAIL PLAN

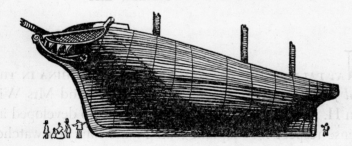

THE "RAINBOW": CONTOURS

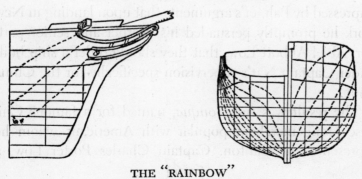

THE "RAINBOW"
BOWS AND BODY PLAN

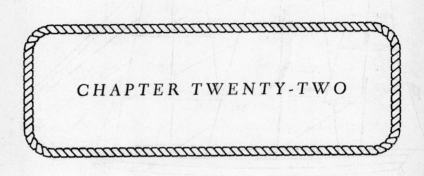

CHAPTER TWENTY-TWO

N AT PALMER, ON HIS VOYAGE HOME FROM CHINA IN THE *Paul Jones* in 1843, took as passengers Mr and Mrs William H. Low. Mr Low was one of many who developed an intense respect for Captain Nat. In the long sea watches they discussed intricacies of ship design, and Low was so impressed by Palmer's arguments that upon landing in New York he promptly persuaded his brother and senior partner, Abiel Abbott Low, that they should order a ship built under Captain Nat's supervision specifically for the China trade.

The result was the *Houqua*, named for a famous Chinese Hong merchant popular with Americans whom he represented at Canton. Captain Charles Porter Low, a third brother, states definitely in his reminiscences that the model of the *Houqua* had been made by Palmer. Captain Nat himself admitted in a letter that he first designed her as a brig for the opium trade, and that the original contract was drawn for a smaller vessel than the one finally produced.

The details have some interest because of an old and profitless argument as to which was the first clipper ship. The *Rainbow* and the *Houqua* were begun at about the same time. Griffiths implies that the *Rainbow* was laid down first. At any rate, she was launched second because of the long delays and doubts of Howland and Aspinwall. The important point is that commercial circumstances—the opening of new treaty ports and relaxation of restrictions at the original Chinese point of trade—made it possible for the two principal contributors to fast-sailing design to try out their theories, unimpeded, beginning at almost the same moment. Palmer had taken a hand in the designing of the Dramatic packets, but there is no adequate evidence that he was the sole designer. In the case of the *Houqua* he appears to have had full control over details of design.

That is how the history of inventions usually works out. Individual men have bright ideas, but they have to wait for events to produce a demand for their ideas. The events themselves usually have altered the ideas, helping to shape them. To say that either Griffiths or Palmer "invented" the clipper is to give too easy an answer to a complicated question. Griffiths by mathematics, Palmer by hunch, had been working along different routes toward the same goal. A sponsor with more money than caution might have given either one of them the chance to apply his theories years earlier, but it took the prospect of large profits in a new trade to get them their backers at the same time.

Neither the *Houqua* nor the *Rainbow* was a clipper in the meaning of the word as it was spoken in the Eighteen Fifties. Neither one was a packet as the word was understood in the Eighteen Thirties. The *Rainbow*, on her first homeward voyage, made a maximum speed of 14 knots, which so far as I have been able to discover was the top speed for any ship up to the year 1846, but it was only a trifle faster than the top speed recorded by the best of the frigates. Several such experimental ships had to be built before the right proportions of the much-altered model could be balanced up for best effect. Time also was needed for skippers accustomed to older craft to learn how best to handle them. On the *Rainbow's* maiden voyage, despite a record for the whole run out and back, she did not come near the homeward-bound time of such flat-floored ships as the *Natchez*. Her outward voyage required 108 days, the homeward one 102.

On the *Rainbow's* second China voyage, Captain Land was getting the hang of her, learning to use less sail on the foremast. (Griffiths, profiting by experience, was to step the foremast relatively farther aft in his next ship.) Land, after only two weeks in the port of New York to discharge and load cargo, took the *Rainbow* out again to Hongkong in 99 days, and home in 84. The difference must be partly credited to the favorable monsoon, another factor which should always be taken into account in comparing China voyages.

There is a belt of chronic calms lying roughly around the equator, centering somewhat to the north of it. In the open ocean, below those calms or doldrums, the winds blow at a fairly steady rate all year from points of the compass lying between south and east. North of the doldrums there is a similar belt of northeast trade winds. In most parts of the world, north of the northeast trades and south of the southeast trades, the winds blow erratically from the west, alternating light breezes and gales. But inland conditions on the great continent of Asia disturb both the northeast trades and the westerlies. The Asian plateau, in its cold season, sends chilly air sliding downhill and out to sea. In the hot season the warmed air rises up the mountainsides. This special movement of air causes the northeast trades to extend farther north off the China coast, in winter, than they do elsewhere. In summer it pulls the trades into reverse. Thus the passage down the China Sea for a sailing ship always has been much easier in the winter months than in the summer ones.

Most of the sea-borne trade along the south and east coasts of Asia, from time out of mind, has been conducted in vessels that did not attempt to make more than one round voyage a year. They let the winds blow them to their destination on one monsoon, and there waited for the monsoon to reverse itself with the seasons and blow them home again. Such ships as the *Rainbow* must have seemed miraculous to observers in eastern waters. She made two complete voyages round the world and back in little more than a year. Their junks attempted only one round voyage a year down the two or three thousand miles of the China Sea to the East Indies and home again.

This breaking of the old cycle of one China voyage a year was a stronger reason than ever for making ships sharp and weatherly. Before the Eighteen Forties, China merchants in England and America always had tried to attune their sailings to the monsoons. When difficulties in port at the other end caused a ship to miss the monsoon it was considered a catastrophe. But ships built on Griffiths' principles proved themselves capable of beating their way down the China Sea against the unfavorable monsoon, losing only a week or so in accomplishing what the junks never had attempted at all.

The *Rainbow*, on her second voyage, had come within 16 days of completing a passage to China and back in the elapsed time of six months. Captain Land, who seldom opened his mouth except to bellow orders that all but blew his second mate off the weather earing, announced definitely that it would be impossible to build a faster ship.

The *Houqua* had been doing almost as well. She proved herself consistently able to make the China run in either direction in about 90 to 100 days, as compared with the expected time of 120 days or more, taken by ordinary "fast" ships. Her steadily fine performance is perhaps more significant than the faster single passages of some ships that also had runs slower than the *Houqua's* worst.

While the pioneers, Griffiths and Palmer, were making these notable advances in ship design, Donald McKay continued on a methodical route that gave every promise of solid success, but hardly a glimmer of brilliance. Even his younger brother Lauchlan had won earlier notice, by publishing in 1839 the first systematic work by an American on the science of shipbuilding.

Lauchlan, much the more mercurial of the two, had quickly mastered shipbuilding and then had gone for a cruise as "chips" in a naval vessel. He continued to dabble at shipbuilding off and on, but most of the time he preferred a finished ship to one on the stocks. There have been few men in all history who could drive one with such speed and assurance. His book on the methods of shipbuilding, useful and valuable as it was, contains no new ideas. It is a competent exposition of methods as he had learnt them in the early Eighteen Thirties, and of the principles then thought trustworthy. The plates which illustrate it were old-fashioned by the time they appeared; but that was true of everything written on the subject, throughout the better part of the clipper ship era, with the sole exception of the works of John Willis Griffiths.

Brady's *Kedge Anchor*, an extremely popular manual of seamanship, gives never a hint in its eighth edition of 1855 that there had been any change in ship design for thirty years, or that such a thing as a clipper ever existed. This was not merely a reprint of the first edition of 1847. It was labeled, "Improved and Enlarged." Popular magazines of the Fifties carried woodcuts and steel engravings showing promptly the obvious changes in design brought about by Palmer and Griffiths, but technical manuals with hardly an exception continued for many years after the clipper-ship era to illustrate the typical ship as a packet of about 1833 or a frigate of 1812.

This is worth noting, because the public at large was slow to realize *why* things were happening, in the shipyards, in the way in which they *were* happening. The United States Navy was even slower. Brady was a sailing master in the navy, which probably accounts for his conservatism. But it must be remembered that there were hundreds of old-fashioned ships still afloat for every clipper before 1850, and that the man in the street had been talking about fast ships for a long time, meaning American clipper schooners and packets. The nature of the refinements which began the last great change in naval architecture was probably of no more immediate interest to the general public than the hidden changes are, nowadays to us, that give a new car a few miles an hour greater top speed.

Most American ships always had been fast, compared with most foreign ones. Captain John Land evidently thought the limit had been reached with 14 knots. To arm-chair sailors, with less reason than Land had for knowing what it took to squeeze that last extra knot off the reel, the slight advance of the *Houqua* and the *Rainbow* over their predecessors may not have seemed phenomenal. Everything was moving rapidly, in the Eighteen Forties, but ordinary men still clung to their ordinary ways.

That must be understood if we are to account for the early career of Donald McKay as an independent ship-builder. Unquestionably McKay knew what Griffiths and Palmer were up to. Yet he plugged quietly along during the pioneering Eighteen Forties, building the ships men asked him to build, building them very well indeed, but contributing nothing basic to the art.

At the age of twenty-nine, McKay had encountered his only early setback. Jacob Bell had got him an important post at the Brooklyn Navy Yard. But American mechanics, at about that time, were beginning to fear the effect of immigration upon their own jobs. For shipwrights, this was a short-sighted view. Immigrants had to come in ships, and immigration kept the shipyards busy. Nevertheless, the native Americans at the Navy Yard refused to work under a Nova Scotian, and hounded McKay out of the yard.

Mr Bell stood by his former employee and promptly sent him to Maine to oversee the construction of some vessels at Wiscasset. What he saw there of the methods of the "no mistake Down Easters," as they smugly called themselves in a popular song, taught the young master shipwright where opportunity really lay. The organization of shipwright labor into separate trades had proceeded rapidly during his thirteen years in New York yards. The old-style craftsman who could do a little of anything, and who wasted a lot of time switching from job to job, had gradually evolved into a specialist. The improvised "shears," rigged when needed to handle heavy timbers, had been replaced, in New York, by permanent derricks. These too were by comparison great time-savers. Lathes and power saws had come into use, as well as improved forging methods. The first flicker of efficiency engineering was noticeable, along the East River in New York, in the exciting Eighteen Thirties of the packet ships.

McKay, bringing these ideas to Maine, was looked upon as a miracle man. Down East writers, indeed, credit him with having invented in the Eighteen Forties many of the gadgets which he had learnt about in New York, and which he was the first to employ at a New England port. This is not surprising. The New York yards that built the famous packets were years ahead of any others on earth. That was another reason why Old England found it difficult to compete. The nearness of standing timber usually has been the chief advantage of any shipbuilding area, but that does not account for New York's pre-eminence in the Eighteen Thirties and Forties. Most of the important timber, by that time, was being brought by sea from the Carolinas and the coast of Maine. New York's secret was the idea of efficiency, the gospel of speed and co-ordination, during the making as well as in the use of the product. When these methods were introduced by McKay and others to sections of the coast nearer to the standing timber supply, New York's importance as a center of wooden shipbuilding quickly declined, and Maine within a few years became the center of the industry.

The fact that Donald McKay was sent to supervise vessels being built in Maine for New York account, under contract with a New York builder, indicates the trend of events. For one thing, the New York yards were rushed to capacity. For another, New York capital was reaching out and seeking new investment areas. New York continued to build the finest ships for the luxury trades, and these were worth their higher relative cost per ton. But when contracts for ordinary cargo carriers came to such men as Jacob Bell, in the late Thirties and early Forties, they were aware that the work could be done more economically where the timber actually grew.

McKay, returning down the coast, stopped off at Newburyport and got a job overseeing the completion of the ship *Delia Walker*, which was already on the stocks when he first saw her. The new foreman's method of organizing the laborers so impressed the yard's owner, John Currier, Jr, that he offered McKay a five-year contract.

That was the signal for which Donald McKay had been waiting. If his value was so obvious that another man wished to bind him for five years as a subordinate, it should be as obviously valuable to an outright partner. He soon found his partner in the person of another Currier named William, and the firm of Currier & McKay hung out its shingle on the upper reaches of a stretch of sloping shoreline at the mouth of the Merrimac River.

There was nothing very notable about the new firm's first two products, the bark *Mary Broughton*, 323 tons, and the ship *Ashburton*, 449 tons. Both were built to the order of Down East owners, and Down Easters still unalterably loved a codfish head and a mackerel tail. Currier & McKay, to show what they could do, had to wait for a commission from the more enlightened regions to the southwestward. Presently, from Andrew Foster & Son of New York, came an order for a fast little ship for the coffee trade.

The result was the *Courier*, launched in 1842. Her tonnage was 392. McKay modeled her himself specifically for the trade for which she was intended, and his success is vouched for by the same Captain Charles Porter Low who later sailed in the *Houqua*. Low called the *Courier* "very fast" when he wrote of her in his book of "recollections."

The dispositions of Currier and McKay do not seem to have been harmonious, for they dissolved their partnership after a year or so. Captain Arthur H. Clark says they divided everything equally, even cutting the moulds and models in two with a saw.

CHAPTER TWENTY-THREE

Down Easters who pridefully claim McKay as one of them overlook the fact that with hardly an exception the ships with which he advanced the art of marine architecture had to be built for New Yorkers, or for Englishmen, or at his own risk. McKay, born in Nova Scotia and trained in New York, carried his strange, slowly developing genius to Massachusetts in 1840 and quickly became one of the foremost builders of the state. But it is very much more than probable that his Down East neighbors and clients, far from contributing to his success in any way of which their descendants can be justly proud, actually retarded his development by many years.

He was not a product of the region, and the region

taught him nothing. He left New York just before the most exciting days in that port's yards began. Had he stayed a little longer he might well have kept pace with Griffiths and Palmer in the basic development of fast-sailing models. But he seems to have been content to give the Down East owners what they wanted in the way of design and to concentrate his undoubtedly great genius for several years upon problems of procedure and craftsmanship, without much regard for improvement in the lines of his products. He was steadily busy. It is possible that because of this he was out of touch with the new developments which were coming so swiftly on South Street, Manhattan Island.

Here again, the hard facts of trade and economics had a good deal to do with the individual man's chance to use his own ideas. McKay had cast his lot with the Down Easters. The Down East ports were not able either to export or to import as large cargoes as had become the rule in New York City. The Erie Canal and a growing network of railroads had made New York the logical ocean port for a vast and rapidly developing region east of the Mississippi. New England had no easy outlet to the main trade route westward, on and south of the Great Lakes. As a consequence, Boston and the other near-by ports of the eastern seaboard supplied imports to a region only 150 miles or so inland, and drew the products from the same region for shipment to other markets. New York was doing that job, by 1840, for a region 1000 miles deep.

It made a difference. A ship bringing 20,000 bolts of British-made cotton cloth into Boston harbor would find individual dealers able to handle only a few hundred bolts apiece. In New York, a single firm might promptly buy the whole shipment and send it off in batches to twenty different inland cities for resale. There was no such group of inland cities to which the Boston merchants could conveniently and profitably distribute their imports. Such a large shipment, at the port of Boston, would probably glut the market. Prices would be forced down by the effort to sell it off quickly, and nobody would profit.

These circumstances made it advisable for Boston merchants to bring in smaller cargoes of everything in which they traded, and smaller ships were the rule. Experience had shown also that too large a vessel, when loading at Boston, might be tied up for months while receiving a full cargo in many small consignments. When such a ship was waiting and empty, merchants were not eager to be the first to put goods aboard her, knowing that their money would be tied up too, for a long time, before she could complete a cargo and sail.

Such were the reasons lying behind Bostonian reluctance to order big ships from McKay. They do not excuse the Bostonian stubbornness in clinging to outmoded models. If the right rule for Boston was small cargoes and frequent sailings, then the faster the ships the better.

The success of the little coffee-ship *Courier* got prompt recognition in New York for the talents of its Newburyport builder. David Ogden commissioned him in 1843 to build the *St George*, 845 tons. This was a considerable tribute as she was to be the first ship of a projected line of Red Cross packets. Ogden's "saints line" ran too irregularly to be classed with its punctual competitors. I have so far been unable to discover anything to indicate that the *St George*, built with a new partner named Pickett, made any notable records.

In 1844 an order came to McKay for a large packet for the Red Star line to Liverpool. Donald McKay and his new partner set to work on the *John R. Skiddy*, 980 tons, and launched her early in 1845. She proved to be consistently fast but not phenomenal. Her best westbound passage was 25 days as compared with the 17 days of the much older *Caledonia*, a considerably smaller packet, or the 16-day record of the slightly larger and earlier *Yorkshire*. The *John R. Skiddy's* average of 32 days for the westward run, however, was surpassed by no other Liverpool packet afloat at the time of her launch, excepting the famous *Yorkshire*, which hung up the unapproached record of 29 days average for the uphill passage over a period of 18 years of continuous service. The *John R. Skiddy's* record covers five years only, as she was wrecked in 1850.

Up to 1844, McKay had worked quietly, allowing his products and methods to advertise themselves. His first noteworthy reward came in that year: Dennis Condry, whose ship the *Delia Walker* had been completed by McKay at Newburyport, had a chance to put in a good word for the young builder where it would count most. Enoch Train of Boston was en route to Europe to arrange for the establishment of an English terminus for the first packet line out of the port that soon was to call its State House "the hub of the solar system." He chanced to be traveling on the same ship with Condry. If his line was to have a chance of succeeding, Mr Train knew that he would have to order ships "on the New York model." He would have preferred, he said regretfully, to commission a Boston builder to produce the ships for Boston's own first packet line.

Mr Condry admitted that no builders in Boston proper could match the packet-ship genius of the New York yards. But he mentioned a New York trained, exceptionally competent young shipbuilder a few miles up the coast in Newburyport who could not only build ships on the New York model, but had actually received orders for such vessels from New York itself.

Home from Europe, Enoch Train hustled up to Newburyport. Legend has it that he signed a contract for his first packet within less than an hour of his first sight of Donald McKay. The *Joshua Bates*, built in fulfillment of that contract, was something of a comedown for her builder. Her measurement was 620.26 tons. When she was launched, the legend further states, Mr Train was so pleased that he gripped the builder's hand and urged him to move to Boston, promising the necessary financial backing. Carl C. Cutler, a nautical historian who takes all legends with a sufficient quantity of deep-sea salt, has pointed out however that Mr Train was operating on a shoestring at the time, and that McKay's ships probably helped the Train White Diamond Line rather more than the White Diamond orders helped McKay.

In any event, McKay does seem to have moved to Boston at Train's suggestion, and Train did place with McKay orders for nine ships in all, thereafter, at an average rate of one a year. The second and third ships for the White Diamond Line progressively stepped up the size of Boston packets to what had been usual for New York ones in recent years. These two were the *Washington Irving*, 751 tons, and the *Anglo Saxon*, 894 tons.

Enoch Train made an almost single-handed effort to keep pace, at least in size and quality of vessels, with Boston's chief competitor. The task was not made any easier by McKay's first New York packet ship customers, the Skiddys. They soon sent the young Boston builder an order which the operators of the New York yards would have cut one another's throat to get. Donald McKay, aged thirty-six, quietly turned to and built the largest merchant sailing ship in existence, the *New World*, 1404 tons. He built her so beautifully that when she reached New York the principal firm of shipowners in America, Grinnell, Minturn & Company, offered a price for her on sight which the Skiddys thought they could not afford to turn down. McKay built her so well, moreover, that when he himself died at the age of seventy she was still profitably voyaging, and was to continue at work for years longer, in testimony to his enduring craftsmanship.

With a kind of magnificent reluctance, Boston thereafter bought a majority of McKay's ships, although not one of his six greatest record-breakers was to be launched for a Boston firm. Train almost kept up with the pace set by New York when he ordered, late in 1846, the *Ocean Monarch* of 1301 tons. Both she and the *Anglo Saxon* early became victims of marine disaster, and it was not until 1850 that McKay again had so large a vessel to build. In the meanwhile he launched seven ships and two barks for Bostonians, averaging a little over 750 tons apiece, as well as four ships for New York account with an average size 200 tons larger.

While Boston was reacting back toward caution, after Enoch Train's first splurge above the 1000-ton level, the revolution in the New York yards continued. William H. Webb, former fellow-apprentice of McKay, had done astonishing things with the business inherited from his father Isaac. If the younger Webb had bothered to make more explicit public claims, it might be possible to shift to him part of the credit usually given Griffiths and Palmer for pioneering in ship design. Some of those who insist upon choosing a "first" clipper point to the little tea ship *Helena*, launched by Webb in 1841. Her waterlines just missed being hollow, forward. She had somewhat sharper floors, amidships, than the Palmer packets, and a rather long hollow run aft. Her model was well on the way toward that of the true clippers, but she seems to me to have been a packet somewhat refined for the special conditions of the tea trade for which she was specifically built.

Webb, like McKay, concentrated in the Forties upon packets. He build fifteen within the decade. The majority were fast. His *Yorkshire* became the most famous packet afloat. In addition to the *Helena* he also launched the fast-sailing tea-ships *Cohota*, *Montauk*, and *Panama*. Of these, the *Montauk* was especially speedy. Her first four homeward runs from China were made in from 87 to 90 days apiece. By 1847 Webb was building big steamers as well as packets. It can be argued that two of the mechanical peculiarities of these early self-propelled vessels influenced the design of the clippers which came a few years afterward.

One characteristic of most ships built before Eighteen Hundred had been the "tumble home" [1] of the topsides, a

----

[1] See illustration, top of page 207.

feature of design influenced somewhat by the tonnage laws, somewhat by mistaken notions of safety and buoyancy. A pronounced tumble home is noticeable in all British naval craft as late as the Eighteen Sixties, but the error had been corrected in the merchant service before that. This came about largely because of the difficulty of locating paddle wheels on the early steamships. Screw propellers were in use on small steamboats in the late Thirties, but the paddle wheel was relied upon for propulsion in most of the large ocean steamers until 1858, when the *Great Eastern* was launched with both paddle boxes and screw.

If paddle wheels were to be attached to a typical ship with pronounced tumble home, the upper parts of the paddle boxes were necessarily very wide, presenting a considerable resistance to head winds. Paddle wheels and boxes also were proved, by early experience, to be very liable to damage from large waves. The more strongly and compactly the boxes could be built, the better. Consequently, the tumble-home amidships was soon eliminated, leaving only enough clearance for the actual blades of the paddles. This straightening of the topsides was found to have no bad effect, while it increased considerably the carrying capacity of the ships.

The other possible contribution of paddle-wheel steamers to ship design was the influence they had upon the location of the dead flat, or widest part of the vessel. It was best to locate the thrust of the paddles at a point where the water being forced aft would not meet any unnecessary resistance from the hull. Therefore they were placed at the widest part. This also was most convenient for the location of boilers and machinery, and for the coal bunkers. But as the steamers increased in speed it was found that the action of the bows upon the water made a bow wave which traveled along with the vessel and which produced a permanent trough at just the point where the paddles should be taking their strongest bite into the water. By moving them farther aft, the next natural wave was built up under the wheels themselves.[1] This made it advisable both to sharpen the bows in order to reduce the turbulence of the bow waves, and to move the dead flat to a point approximately amidships.

Fortunately for sailing ship design, some of the early steamers proved unprofitable. Their engines were taken out and their sail plans increased. It was then found that they sailed all the better because of the changes in hull design originally dictated by the problem of placing the paddle boxes where they would work best.

This influence was probably not a major one. Sailing ships at the same time were gradually being altered in the same way. It was all part of the trend which swiftly, during the Eighteen Forties, was revising all the basic concepts of what a good ship should look like. The fact that the pioneering was done almost entirely in New York City can be explained in part in yet another way. Always it has been a custom for different parts of the world's coast lines to produce characteristic models particularly suited to the conditions of near-by waters, or to the kinds of voyages profitable for local shipowners. In the early years of the last century, typical whalers were built in the New Bedford region, West Indiamen in Baltimore and thereabouts, East India-

[1] See illustrations of *Great Western* and *Great Eastern*, page 45-46.

men at Boston and Salem, Western Ocean packets in New York.

"The New York model," for many years, meant a packet, and the early regular packet lines had flourished only in New York. The name "clipper" had been associated with the clipper schooners of Baltimore. Its new application, to clipper ships, was not clearly understood outside New York until after 1850. The earlier vessels which we now sometimes call clippers, the *Helena* and *Rainbow* and a few others contemporaries, were referred to in newspapers of their day as Canton packets. Therefore, when New York in the Eighteen Forties began to take over more and more of the East Indies and China trade which had formerly centered at Boston, the ships built for the purpose were described as "sharp ships on the New York model." It took some time for other ports to realize that the distinction was something more than local, that a scientific revolution in ship design occurring in three or four yards on South Street, would shake the great industry on the far away Clyde, and force imitation even in hidebound, pridebound Boston.

The fast New York model was more than an adaptation, for the reason that New York really had become what Boston in her declining glories was to claim to be: the hub of the universe of shipping. New Yorkers had adventured into all trades with all places. As from Liverpool and London, their ships went everywhere, on all kinds of errands. But Liverpool and London, under the last blighting years of the Navigation Laws, had yet to awaken.

It would be unfair to neglect William H. Webb in any appraisal of the great days of the Forties that led up so swiftly to the ultimate clippers. Webb produced more notably fast wooden ships than any other builder in the world, except McKay himself, and Webb was building very fast ones long before McKay's reputation was based upon anything more than the virtue—worthy in itself—of sound workmanship.

CHAPTER TWENTY-FOUR

SOME HAVE CLAIMED THAT THE CLIPPER-SHIP ERA started with the *Ann McKim*, a big Baltimore "schooner" of 1833, rigged as a ship. Others have given the *Helena*, the *Houqua*, the *Montauk*, the *Rainbow*, credit for being the first clipper ship. These four, launched between 1841 and 1845, all show traces of a movement toward the real thing.

We may as well admit that the first clipper is a myth, and begin with an unarguable fact: no-one seems to have taken the trouble to deny that with the launching of the *Sea Witch* the clipper-ship era triumphantly got under way. Call her the first fully recognizable clipper if you like, or the first great one. She may have been the former. She

[237]

certainly was the latter. Howland & Aspinwall, impressed by the excellent performance of the *Rainbow*, had given John Griffiths a free hand, with specific orders on one point only: he was to produce for them the fastest ship afloat, and he did.

Although she was the earliest of the great clippers, and one of the smallest, there is no other whose career demonstrates so variously and well the whole sweep of clipper-ship achievement. She figured in most of the important clipper-ship trades, excepting only the Australian run which in general called for bigger vessels. She was launched at just the time when the word "clipper" was beginning to have a special recognizable meaning in New York, as applied to full-rigged ships. Her life span—ten years and a few months—covered the heroic age of clipper-ship activity in America. She was the perfect expression of one of the two early concepts of fast-sailing design, the culmination of Griffiths' theories in their original unmodified form. A few years later, the Griffiths and Palmer schools of modeling were to blend into the ultimate perfection of the clippers of the Fifties. Yet there are some naval architects today who contend, in the light of all succeeding experience and scientific investigation, that the form of the *Sea Witch* was not noticeably improved upon in the later and faster vessels, but that the greater speed of some of her successors can be credited entirely to their much greater size and consequent ability to carry more sail.

I am not going to tell over again here, in any detail, the story of Griffiths' masterpiece—because I have already put as much of the truth about it as I could discover into a novel called *The Sea Witch*. Here are a few of the facts:

She was launched on December 8th, 1846, from the yard of Smith & Dimon on South Street in New York. The New York *Herald* referred to her next day as, "The splendid ship *Sea Witch*, whose peculiar model and sharp bows have for the past few months attracted so much attention." Her length, on deck, was 170.3 feet, her beam 33.11 feet, and her depth 19 feet. Her tonnage was registered at 907.53. Over all, her length was 192 feet. The most quickly obvious thing about her, as the *Herald* noted, was Griffiths' treatment of the bows. They were definitely hollow at the waterline, and flared outward above water to a degree then considered remarkable. But most unusual of all, Griffiths had omitted the sacred "trail boards."

These formerly useful parts of a ship's structure had become ornamental at best, and at worst had survived as a little extra stiffening for a "head" made insufficiently strong in itself. In ships of around 1800, the fayed timbers of the stem had extended upward and far outward. In some cases they reached as much as ten feet forward of the line where the planksheer—the real hull itself—ended. That massive extra chunk of timber was practically useless except as a counterweight and a perch for the figurehead. Griffiths, as I have already pointed out, had carried his planksheer in the *Rainbow* outward up the curve of the stem's head, inclosing the larger part of that useless timber inside the structure of the bows, and thus achieving greater strength with increased resistance to any downward plunge when the ship pitched.

Turn back to the illustrations on pages 207, 215. The Indiaman, the *Philadelphia*, and the *Rainbow* show the gradual shrinking of the useless "head" and its trail boards.

A little later, Griffiths was to argue that the planksheer both fore and aft should be brought as close as possible to the outer edge of the stem and sternpost. "Inclosing the ship's backbone within the ship's skin," was his way of expressing it.

In the *Sea Witch* he went far toward doing this, and produced the first outright clipper bow. Some of the steamers of the late Thirties, as well as the pilot boats built by Webb and others, had carried the planking forward in somewhat the same manner. Small craft without figureheads for some time had been doing without trail boards. But the *Sea Witch* was the first full-sized merchantman to do away with these hangovers of a theory of structure which Griffiths had successfully argued out of existence. After the *Sea Witch*, fewer and fewer trail boards were seen on American clippers. They persisted as mere ornamentation of British vessels throughout the British clipper era, and are still seen on some yachts. But in 1846, in New York, John Griffiths did without them and produced a hull that nakedly displayed in evident lines the reasoning behind its own structure.

It is interesting to note that the ratio of length to breadth—measuring length on deck and not over-all—had passed the 5 to 1 mark with the *Rainbow*, and with the *Sea Witch* was increased still further to 5.14 to 1.

Under Captain Robert H. Waterman, one of the supermen who did as much as the ships themselves to establish the records of all clippers, the *Sea Witch* sailed for Canton two days before Christmas, 1846. A quick summary of her career and of her first voyage is given so ably in the best general history of the clipper-ship era that I shall quote it without attempting any embellishments. Carl C. Cutler, in *Greyhounds of the Sea*, writes, "Thus started a sea career of less than ten years, by all odds the most remarkable ten years of sail in the history of the world. Before her brief life had ended, the *Sea Witch* had broken more records than a ship of her inches ever had broken and in company with other clippers had established the majority of sailing records that still survive."

Later in his book he picks the story up again: "The *Sea Witch* herself gets back to New York the 25th of July, a trifle over 81 days from Canton, *against the monsoon—*a record. But she has too many records for one more or one less to matter. On her outward passage she passed the Cape of Good Hope 42 days out, having sailed 8894 miles, an average of 206 miles a day for six consecutive weeks—a record. She passed Java Head 70 days and 10 hours out—a record. Her best day's run up to that point was 302 miles, and she averaged 248 miles a day for 10 days.

"On her return she ran from Anjier to the Cape in 26 days, another record. Her best day's run was 312 miles. She took her New York pilot on, 62 days from Anjier, again a record, and during that run she had averaged 264 miles a day for ten days." It should be remembered that those were sea miles, 15 per cent longer than land miles. Freighters that can do as well with steam, day in and day out, are still uncommon. And the *Sea Witch* was a freighter.

Reading that report in the public press, New York went suddenly mad with clipper-ship fever. Nat Palmer, while the *Sea Witch* was performing these miracles, had been superintending the construction of the *Samuel Russell*, a ship slightly larger and admittedly built to beat her. That he had been influenced by Griffiths is proved by the published report which said: "Her bow is formed according to the new style, no lumbering heavy cut-water, the planking running chuck up to the stem."

A further influence is evident in the fact that Captain Nat, a practical man who always had been willing to form opinions on the basis of observed results, had departed in the *Samuel Russell* from his former insistence upon a flat floor. He gave her a considerable, although not an extreme, dead rise. He had his reasons, apart from the proofs established by the *Rainbow*. No-one seriously doubted, by that time or ever afterward, that the flat floor was best for heavy-weather sailing. But size and the nature of the cargo had something to do with the effectiveness of a flat floor. A light and shallow vessel of small size, if made flat, would have a greater tendency to be blown sidewise than would one of the same length and breadth if it were built deep and loaded down with heavy cargo. A flat-floored 70-foot schooner might be designed to draw only three or four feet of water. But another schooner identical to all appearances above water might be drawing eight or ten feet. The one which would be better, for any given trade, would depend upon the cargo and the winds. The deeper one would make less leeway and would stand harder driving. The shallow one might skim along much faster before an exactly favoring wind, but it would be much less handy with the wind abeam, and practically useless with the wind ahead.

One reason, then, for the old sharp V-bottom of early fast-sailing design was the effort to get an adequate amount of depth in comparatively small vessels to prevent leeway or side-slip. As ships became larger, they automatically acquired an adequate depth. The V-form, which contributed greater depth for the same capacity, in comparison with the flat-bottom, became less and less necessary. But in the China trade, the characteristic cargoes were very light. A full load of tea would weigh only one-quarter as much as a full load of flour, or manufactured cloth. The masts of a lightly loaded ship might lie far over from the vertical, even in a moderate wind, a trait called "crankness" which was both inefficient and dangerous. To prevent his ship from being crank with such light cargo, a tea clipper's captain had to carry a good deal of ballast even when he had a full manifest and a deck load. It was the purpose of the ballast to lower the center of gravity well below the center of flotation.

The handiest ballast was stone, but sometimes pig iron or pig lead could be carried as part of the cargo. Whatever kind was chosen, the ballast was concentrated as close as possible to the keel except in the rare cases of ships that were too stiff.

Under these special circumstances a V-shaped bottom had its advantages. It gave adequate depth in spite of light cargo, and the ballast could be crowded into the V, close to the keel, leaving a flat surface for the regular cargo on top of the ballast itself.

Consequently, for ships of moderate size engaged in the China trade, some degree of dead rise was justified—and it is still justified under similar circumstances. In considering the early arguments for and against this feature of design, it is well to remember that the argument itself started in days when a ship measuring over 500 tons was a rarity. Most of the famous clippers were from three to five times as large as that. They got the necessary depth and stability merely by being big enough, and did not have to sink a V-shaped bottom with special ballast to prevent leeway and crank behavior.

The *Samuel Russell*, except for the dead rise introduced to make her more suitable for a special trade, was a logical outgrowth of the packet school of design in which Nat Palmer had excelled all along. That she was a kind of inspired compromise is indicated by her comparative success later when she was shifted from a light-weather trade to a heavy-weather one. She was not quite the match of the *Sea Witch* in either the China or California runs, but she did very well indeed and became famous in both. Nat Palmer himself took her out to China on her maiden voyage and came home in 83 days: excellent sailing.

Throughout the latter Forties, New York clippers continued to be built primarily for the China trade. Smith & Dimon launched the *Memnon* in 1847, the first clipper of more than 1000 tons. She registered 1068. Nat Palmer, two years later, supervised at Bell's yard the construction of the *Oriental*, famous as the clipper that awakened London River to the fact that the waves no longer were ruled exclusively by Britannia. The *Oriental* measured just over 1000 tons as well.

At about the time when the keel of Palmer's new flyer was being laid, the already world-famous *Sea Witch* completed her most spectacular job of sailing. She entered New York harbor on March 25th, 1849, exactly 74 days 14 hours from Hongkong—an all-time world's record from any China port to any port in the North Atlantic, for any kind of cargo carrier, sail or steam, via the Cape of Good Hope. Through storm and calm, day and night, she had averaged better than 9 statute miles an hour for the entire homeward voyage. For the best 10 days in a row, her *average* speed was 12¾ statute miles an hour. She had kept up a speed of 10 statute miles an hour all the way across the Pacific, 10,417 miles, from Peru to China. Bigger and sharper clippers were soon engaged in the same trade, but the record voyage of the *Sea Witch* has stood for nearly a hundred years, unbeaten.

Before 1850, New York had produced a dozen or more ships that have been claimed as clippers, four of them genuinely famous in the history of seafaring, and at least one that can lay a strong claim to having been the most variously excellent wooden ship ever built. In Boston, on New Year's Day of 1850, Donald McKay had two big packets in frame and no clippers in evidence, except on paper.

Some Bostonians knew what was happening, but they regarded it as a brief fad. The craze for speed would wear itself out. Big ships would go begging for cargoes as soon as the new China trade had settled down on a sane basis. So they predicted, and they might have been right in that prediction, had it not been for the gold grains seen glittering in the bottom of Sutter's mill race in 1848.

Here again an accident of commercial history provided very suddenly the special financial conditions under which the long plans of the dreamers and the hunches of the practical observers could have a chance of being tried out in action. Hordes of new Californians, turning the soil only

for gold, needed food and other goods in huge quantities—
needed them at once. The value of speed, which had been
emphasized by the tea trade from the new treaty ports, was
enormously increased. Freight rates rocketed to as much
as four times the normal. A dozen of the fastest New York
ships, including several of the new clippers, bucked their
way around Cape Stiff in Forty-Nine, slashing what had
been a six months' voyage down to four months or less.
Most of them paid their entire cost in the first mad voyage,
despite lost top-hamper.

All these, it should be emphasized, were freight ships.
The Forty-Niners themselves, the human beings of the
great migration, took every possible route that promised to
be shorter than the grueling journey around the Horn. A
brisk passenger trade at once developed via the Isthmus of
Panama, ships running back and forth between the North
Atlantic ports and the Isthmus, which itself was crossed
on foot or muleback to the Pacific side where other ships
kept up the shuttle between that point and San Francisco.

Many of the Forty-Niners, although a minority, did go
all the way by sea, but only a handful went by clipper.
The usual practice was the chartering of any old vessel by
a "company" who shared all expenses equally and often
made things difficult for the captain and crew by taking
company votes on questions of navigation. Nevertheless,
the fact that scores of small and moderate-sized vessels
were commissioned by the emigrant companies, all within
a few months of the year 1849, increased greatly the demand for fast ships as freighters. The emigrant craft were
too crowded with men and their belongings to take more

food and other freight than were needed for their own company on the voyage. The withdrawal of these miscellaneous vessels from other routes caused a shortage of carriers for trade generally. This forced the freight rates up in some measure everywhere, if not as much as in the California trade. As a result, orders for all kinds of ships deluged the better-known builders. Owners hastily got rid of their old droghers to Forty-Niners who insisted on starting at once, and then rushed contracts for up-to-date replacements.

This procedure, in 1850, crowded the New York yards with frames of miscellaneous hulls of all kinds. When news came back from California of the fabulous profits of the freight business to the Golden Gate, those who wanted new clippers and wanted them at once had to seek elsewhere for vacant shipways on which to have them built. New York had room to build only three large clippers in that famous year, plus two modest ones and a clipper packet.

In midsummer of 1850, not far from Donald McKay's yard, Down Easters consequently rubbed their eyes at sight of a most peculiar frame raised by Samuel Hall. It was the first clipper that had been on view in New England, either in port or on the ways. The only thing which prevented Hall's friends from thinking he was mad was the fact that she was being built for A. A. Low & Brother of New York. The New Yorkers were notoriously mad on the question of speed. In this case they were even mad enough to have employed an independent designer to draw the plans and make the model. As if that in itself were not

[247]

a sufficiently dangerous break with precedent—relieving the builder, as it seemed to do, of responsibility for the performance of his product—the designer who had been chosen was a youngster twenty-three years of age, Sam Pook.

CHAPTER TWENTY-FIVE

JOHN GRIFFITHS, THE FIRST NOTABLY SUCCESSFUL CIVIL-
ian marine architect, was associated throughout his early
career with a single firm of builders: Smith & Dimon.
Samuel Hartt Pook brought a new element into the profession when he set up as independent consultant to any
owner or builder who might be ready to pay for his services.
When the shrewd firm of A. A. Low & Brother gave him
his first major assignment, the sound of Pook's name was
well known. His father, Samuel Moore Pook, had long
served as naval constructor for the government. The earliest
mention of the younger Pook seems to be the record that
he, as an apprentice of sixteen, made an official copy of
the lines of the sloop of war *Union*. His rise to personal

reputation must have been swift and brilliant. No amount of family pull could have induced a firm of New Yorkers to have a ship of the latest and sharpest model built so far from their point of operations under the supervision of an unknown youngster in Boston.

News came back, via the Isthmus and the electric telegraph from Charleston, of the McKay-built and Boston-owned ship *Reindeer*, 806 tons. She had arrived at San Francisco on April 2nd, reporting 122 net sailing days with a stop at Valparaiso deducted. Bostonians felt better. It was excellent time, perhaps a record. The much bigger New York ship *Memnon* had made the same claim for net sailing time, but the log might well be checked up. The *Reindeer* was a sensibly and substantially built ship. If she could do as well as that, such a monstrosity as Pook's in the Hall yard could be left to the New Yorkers.

That attitude survived for a few weeks. Then came word that Nat Palmer's *Samuel Russell*, Charles Porter Low master, had whipped around the world's windiest corner and dashed up the Pacific to enter the Golden Gate on May 6th in 109 days flat, no deductions, and no special figuring.

Upon hearing that, two Boston firms drummed up enough courage between them to split the risk and gave McKay a free hand at last to mould a vessel specifically for the booming California trade. They wanted her in a hurry, and a hundred days later McKay put her into the water for them. In doing so, he once more launched the largest merchant sailing ship afloat in the world. The *Stag Hound* measured 1534 tons. Curiously, when freed of restrictions upon his own sense of proportion, McKay followed Griffiths to the hilt in a feature which Griffiths himself was soon to abandon, but was cautious about the one which Griffiths increasingly recommended. The *Stag Hound* had the extreme dead rise of 40 inches. But her ends, although they also were very sharp, were not hollow.

Any qualms which McKay may have had about following Griffiths at all were removed while the *Stag Hound* was still on the ways. A report came up the coast that Griffiths' sharp-bottomed, sharp-ended *Sea Witch* had roared down around the Horn and up to San Francisco in 97 days, annihilating all California records by a margin of nearly two weeks.

The Pook-Hall clipper *Surprise*, 1006 tons, startled convention in another way: she went into the water fully rigged. That was on October 5th, 1850. She was built very much in accordance with Griffiths' theories, which Pook had obviously studied with all the eagerness of a young mind impatient with fuddy-duddy traditions. She had 30 inches of dead rise, compared with 40 inches for McKay's still unlaunched *Stag Hound*. The bows of the *Surprise* were less sharp than those of McKay's first California ship; but they were, as Griffiths recommended, distinctly hollow at water line.

The *Surprise*, Dumaresq master, loaded part of her cargo at Boston, took in the rest at New York, and sailed for California December 13th. She arrived in 96 days 15 hours, standing into the Golden Gate a fraction of a day ahead of the record so recently set by the *Sea Witch*. The reputation of Samuel Hartt Pook as a designer was clinched with the first voyage of his first clipper. The *Surprise* had broken what was currently the most important of the world's sailing marks—and had broken it at first try.

The *Stag Hound* sailed from New York on February 1st, 1851, lost her main topmast and all three top-gallant masts in a gale six days out, was expertly put to rights at sea, and continued to California via Valparaiso. She arrived out in 113 days, of which five had been spent at anchor in the Chilean port. Considering the mishap, it was very fast sailing, but McKay had wanted a record and was disappointed.

The *Stag Hound* was an odd production in many ways. McKay had followed Griffiths' advice in removing the hollows from the run aft, but he had not put them forward. Her bows had a very little of the outward flare above water which Griffiths thought so important. Her planksheer was carried up all the way along the stem, with no overhanging head at all. Her dead flat was just aft of amidships. Bold in some features, cautious in others, she was obviously the experiment of a man who had long been hampered by unimaginative clients. No doubt she represented as well a real desire not merely to copy what the most successful designer of the day already had done.

By most standards the *Stag Hound* was a thumping success. For a few weeks she was the biggest merchant sailing ship afloat. Her first trading voyage, round the world via San Francisco and China, achieved in eleven months what most ships would have been lucky to do in eleven years: she had paid her entire building cost, all operating expenses, and a clear profit besides of $80,000.

That accounting spoke a language which the shipowners of Boston could understand to a man. For five years thereafter the Bostonians and the English between them kept Donald McKay so busy that he had no time for orders from New York. It was the *Stag Hound,* undeniably, which rocketed him into local favor and made him able at last to design ships according to his own best judgment. But his own dissatisfaction with her became concretely evident before she was even launched. While she was still on the ways he set to work on an even larger clipper so markedly different in model that I am tempted to believe the *Stag Hound* had been made from old plans already on hand when a rush order came in.

Certainly the new ship, as she shaped up in the early months of 1851, had little in common with the *Stag Hound.* She was to be about 250 tons larger in measurement. Her water lines were slightly hollow forward and aft. She had a pronounced flare to the bows above water as recommended by Griffiths. Her dead flat was precisely amidships. Most significant of all, her dead rise at half floor was 20 inches, exactly one-half as much as McKay had given the preceding vessel. It is perhaps notable that Griffiths' *Treatise on Marine and Naval Architecture* had been published just before McKay set to work to mould this new ship for Enoch Train & Co. In that treatise Griffiths indicated some modifications of his views of 1841. The extreme dead rise of the *Stag Hound* probably had reflected McKay's faith in the early Griffiths theory, so triumphantly expressed in the *Sea Witch.* The sudden and startling drop in dead rise, from 40 inches to 20 inches between two ships for the same trade, provides another reason for suspecting that the *Stag Hound* was built from plans which had been on hand for at least a year or two, whereas the next ship was designed from last-minute information and a rethinking of the whole problem.

At any rate, those who knew ships had no doubts about her promise of excellent performance. Representatives of Grinnell, Minturn & Co. of New York were scouting Down East early in 1851, when the New York yards were still catching up with 1850 orders. They saw the new ship in McKay's yard, and thereupon dropped in at Enoch Train's office to offer $90,000 for her on the stocks.

Following a first burst of enthusiasm, Mr Train may have had a few qualms. Perhaps, as Cutler infers from other information, he was still operating on a shoestring and needed the cash. The *Stag Hound*, on her first voyage, was still unreported, and Mr Train had no means of knowing what a money-maker that big Boston-owned ship was to prove to be. Whatever the reason, or variety of reasons, Enoch Train did something he was to bemoan for the rest of his days. He took a quick profit and sold his ship for $90,000, still unlaunched. Boston's chance to make up in one magnificent example for her repression of McKay's genius thus went glimmering.

The ship sold down the coast in this fashion was the *Flying Cloud*, perhaps the best loved and most widely famous of all sailing ships. In her, as if suddenly inspired with full knowledge and insight, McKay blended Griffiths' and Palmer's theories into an almost perfect balance. A few of McKay's later ships, and one of Pook's, were to cover more miles in a single day than the *Flying Cloud*, at her best. But no other clipper except the *Sea Witch* proved to be so consistently fast under all kinds of circumstances, year in, year out. And the *Flying Cloud* twice bettered the best time of the *Sea Witch* to San Francisco. She should have done so, other things being equal, as she was almost twice as large and was particularly designed for the California trade, while the *Sea Witch* was intended for the somewhat different conditions of the China trade via the opposite hemisphere.

When comparing two such great ships, no-one can confidently say that one design is better than another under all circumstances. Ships, like athletes, can have an all-around excellence, or they can narrowly specialize in only one kind of competition. The *Sea Witch* and the *Flying Cloud,* considering their size, were all-time, all-around champions. Some slightly later and rather bigger ships beat them in specific events. We should expect this for the same reason that would prompt us to bet on a trained two-miler rather than a famous decathlon athlete in a two-mile race. The specialist ought to win in his own specialty, against the man who can do all of a variety of things very well indeed, but perhaps none of them greatly.

It was the same with the great ships. We should judge each on a basis of the builder's intentions. The *Sea Witch,* designed for the China trade, set an all-time world's record in that trade. The *Flying Cloud,* designed for the California trade, did the same thing in its own specialty. The fact that both performed exceptionally well in other trades too makes it seem reasonable to call them the two greatest clippers ever built. On the other hand, if you want to choose the great ships on the basis of a kind of performance in which all had an equal chance, somewhere, at some time, then you must judge them either by the maximum speed actually recorded in any one cast of the log, or by the greatest distance covered in any one day.

Both methods of comparison are valid. The important thing is to remember which is being used, because they do not necessarily mix well. The *Flying Cloud* was not the best ship possible for heavy weather and following seas. For such conditions her dead rise should have been even less than it was. She was an inspired compromise. Her dead rise indicated an angle about halfway between the two extremes of sharpness and flatness recorded for other clippers, but slightly on the flattish side. That probably is a major explanation of her versatility.

On her first voyage out to the Golden Gate, McKay's *Flying Cloud* nipped a full week from the mark set by Pook's *Surprise*. The time was two and a half hours less than 90 days flat. If anything was needed to whip up the frenzy for fast ships, and further to dramatize the California trade, that did it. New York had a quick answer, in the series of new claimants to the title of "biggest sailing ship afloat." She was the *Challenge*, built by Webb and launched only 39 days after the *Flying Cloud*. The New York leviathan measured 2006 tons. Webb gave her what seems to have been the most pronounced dead rise of any large clipper: 42 inches. This is one reason for wondering whether Webb really was the peer of Griffiths and Palmer, Pook and McKay, in advancing the principles of design. The four others had given evidence by this time of their realization that extreme dead rise was never necessary in large ships, and was probably detrimental in the heavy weather of the California run. It is only fair to note, however, that the plans of the Webb ship *Gazelle*, when these were published many years later, carried an explanation that her very extreme dead rise was insisted upon by the owners and modeled against Webb's own wishes. It says, "Mr. Webb always maintained that excessive dead rise of floor was not, but rather flat floor was best to secure high speed."

That defense may well have been in order, as the *Gazelle's* dead rise was fantastically high, even for a middle-sized early clipper. It was more than 50 inches. Yet if Webb was reluctant to give such sharpness to the bottom of a ship of 1244 tons, he does not seem to have raised convincing objections in the case of the *Challenge*. Launched several months later than the *Gazelle*, she had the next largest recorded dead rise of any clipper.

Both of these Webb ships became notorious for bad luck of various sorts. Comparatively fast, they were by no means fast enough to compensate for the small carrying capacity caused by the sharpness of their bottoms. New York did better with the *Trade Wind*, which in turn was the largest clipper afloat for a short time after her launch in August 1851. She measured 2045 tons, and made the California run outward in 103 days.

After losing the beautiful *Flying Cloud* from the roster of Boston ships, Bostonians held onto the other three clippers McKay built for them in 1851. Still experimenting, he gave them bows like the *Flying Cloud's* and longer, flatter floors. The clipper packet *Staffordshire* had a dead rise of 20 inches, the *Flying Fish* 25 inches.

Then, with cash in the bank and theories tested, McKay determined to mould one ship free of even an informal sense of responsibility to others. The only way to do that was to take the full financial risk himself, and he did. To make sure that his fourth try at largest-in-the-world would not be eclipsed by the New Yorkers while she was building, he added at the last minute some extra frames amidships—each an exact duplicate of the dead flat—to bring her out to a measurement of 2421 tons. This procedure, incidentally, also produced a ship with a greater ratio of length to breadth than any predecessor: 5.8 to 1. It is a reminder of one of Colonel Beaufoy's findings of more than fifty years earlier, that an elongation of the midsection of almost any form he tested reduced rather than increased the resistance.

No Bostonian—not even a mad New Yorker—came forward to buy the new colossus while she was on the stocks. The opinion was general that McKay had overreached himself, that there could be no profitable trade for vessels larger than 2000 tons. In a way it is fortunate that McKay got no backing at this particular moment in his career, for it gives us a chance to see his behavior when he was left entirely to his own devices. He had been responsible to no-one for the design of the new ship. He preferred to be responsible to no-one for her operation. After a few days' study of the intricate finances of the ocean freight business, he appointed his trusted brother Lauchlan skipper, and sent the magnificent new *Sovereign of the Seas* down to New York to take on the largest cargo which had ever left that port in a single bottom.

This was an all-McKay enterprise: Donald McKay as designer, builder, owner, operator and consigner, Lauchlan McKay as captain and commercial agent for his brother. Probably it was the first time when a ship with some claim to greatness was both built and operated with no concessions to the hidebound notions which have made "the owners" a continuing nightmare to both builders and skippers throughout all the history of merchant ships.

The *Sovereign of the Seas* had lines very similar to those of the *Flying Cloud*, except that her dead rise was one-third less, or 20 inches, and her length was proportionately greater. The more modest dead rise and consequently fuller midsection may have been McKay's reason for bringing her lines together at the sternpost with a distinctly more hollow run than he had used in the case of the former ship.

The *Sovereign of the Seas* sailed from New York for San Francisco August 4th, 1852. She bucked head winds all the way to the equator, but made that leg of the voyage in the very fast time of 25 days in spite of the weather. Great equinoctial gales racked her off the Horn. When she reached the latitude of Valparaiso in the Pacific, a terrific gust tore away her main topmast, mizzen topgallantmast, and all the canvas off the foremast with the foretopsail yard to boot. Almost any other commander in the world, in that perilous situation, would have followed instantly the rule in all the books. He would have ordered the wreckage cut away lest the vast spars smash the sides of the lurching ship, as it lay helpless and out of control.

But Lauchlan McKay was one of the titans. With a superb confidence and just the right exercise of the remaining sources of power left on the crippled main and mizzen masts, he kept the wreckage clear of the sides while it was being untangled and secured. He saved even the sails, re-rigged without putting into port, and continued for San Francisco. Despite the mishap, the *Sovereign of the Seas* made the season's fastest run to San Francisco, 103 days. Thence she went out to Honolulu and took on 8000 barrels of whale oil.

It was on the return run from Honolulu to New York, deep in the water with cargo, that she became the first vessel to chalk up more than 400 sea miles in a day. Nothing afloat, under sail or steam, ever had done it before. This event ushered in the heroic high four years of sailing-ship history.

CHAPTER TWENTY-SIX

THERE ARE ONLY THIRTEEN OCCASIONS ON RECORD WHEN a sailing ship has sailed more than 400 sea miles in twenty-four hours by the clock. As described earlier in this book, the *Sovereign of the Seas* was first to achieve the 400-mile mark, between noon of March 17th, 1853, and the following mid-day. Four years and a day later, in another equinoctial gale, another Donald McKay product, the *Lightning*, logged 430 miles noon to noon. No sailing ship built outside New England has ever covered more than 400 sea miles in a day. No steamer that could keep up such a pace in deep water was to be launched for a generation.

Yet between March 1853 and March 1857, runs of

better than 400 sea miles a day were made thirteen times under sail, and on twelve of those miraculous occasions the ships had been launched from the East Boston yard of the same craftsman, Donald McKay. Only young Pook was able to model a vessel capable of entering this company of clipper ship giants, upon which McKay ships otherwise have an exclusive monopoly. Pook's *Red Jacket* sailed 413 miles on January 19th, 1854. The other claimants to this rarest of marine triumphs were McKay's *Flying Cloud*, *Great Republic*, and *Donald McKay*, each of which did it once, his *Sovereign of the Seas* with two such performances, his *Lightning* with three, and his *James Baines* with four.

These years of the middle Fifties of the last century obviously were turbulent, untypical ones. International trade and finance were knocked out of kilter and made to boom fantastically by the great migration to California and by the Australian gold rush that began just when the Californian excitement was beginning to taper off. Unusual conditions called for unusual ships, and for feats of seamanship unheard of in other periods.

Sound nautical historians caution us that the ships which sprang into being by the scores to meet such unusual conditions were in themselves as distorted as the times which produced them. Some claim flatly that the clippers as a class were not well designed, were absurd freaks.

Their claim is nonsense. I have tried throughout this book to show why. The successful product in any field and at any time is the one that best does what is expected of it. The great clippers did that, while they were needed, in a very extraordinary time. When they were no longer needed, they vanished. It is certainly a mistake to claim, as some misguided enthusiasts have done, that the clippers were products of a lost art which men have been trying ever since to equal.

I think the clippers represent instead an almost super-human triumph in bridging two epochs of human development that did not quite manage to come neatly together in the process of history. The new mechanical science of the Industrial Revolution was unable to keep up with the new conditions of life which it created. There was a gap of about a decade during which the world called for steam-ship performance, as we now think of steamship perform-ance, and the new kinds of mechanics were not yet able to provide it. In that decade the old style mechanics, the geniuses of the sailing ships, seized upon the new scientific principles and applied them triumphantly to one of the oldest of human machines. If their products were absurd freaks, as some good modern marine architects say, then they were the sort of absurd freaks which do the job that has to be done when the "proper" device proves wanting.

Donald McKay, on two or three occasions, seems to have jumped in advance of even the demands of those furious years. But each time he did it at his own risk, and only a tragedy which was to befall his hugest product pre-vents us from saying that his foresight was always justified.

After 1851 the clippers came from the ways in such numbers that it would be confusing to keep track of them in any book of this length. Those who want to read the full story of the great ships can find it in Carl C. Cutler's splendid history, *Greyhounds of the Sea*. Cutler lists 54 ships built in 1851 that deserve to be called clippers, and

75 launched in 1852. The following year brought 120 from the ways. Thereafter the number declined again. By 1856 the world emergency which demanded such remarkable vessels was over. To take the evidence from another aspect, Pook was the only man except McKay himself who ever modeled a clipper larger than the *Sovereign of the Seas*. This seems to indicate that normal demands of trade, even in the boom years, called for a maximum size of around 2000 tons. The majority of the famous clippers from other yards measured between 1200 and 2000.

Yet McKay, with a whole series of ships, exceeded that practical upper limit. This brings up the interesting and never wholly answered question: Does the great man mould his own times, or do the times shape the great man? In McKay's case the answer seems to be: A little of both. The times, as they affected Boston, made McKay produce ships throughout the Eighteen Forties that were not the ships he would have liked to build. Then suddenly, when his genius broke free in 1851 with the *Flying Cloud*, he himself began to shape the times. He was ahead of his own clients, so far ahead that on at least five occasions he built big ships on his own account, entirely at his own risk, confident that their behavior would find them a quick market.

The first time he did this the speculation was extremely successful. The *Sovereign of the Seas* paid her builder $135,000 profit in her first complete voyage of nine months. This record so impressed the New York ship brokers that McKay was able to sell her for more than he would have asked before she was launched.

In less than a year McKay built five more splendid ships,

[264]

none so large as the *Sovereign of the Seas* but all rated as extreme clippers and three of them over 2000 tons in measurement. Then once more, and magnificently, he let go. The *Great Republic*, launched in October of 1853, measured 4555 tons. No other wooden ship has ever approached her size. The mere problem of making so much timber hold together in one piece, when hurled about in a Cape Horn hurricane, was colossal, considering the hull alone. Add to that the terrific strain of masts over a yard in diameter towering to an average height of 200 feet above deck. In fair weather they spread enough canvas between them to cover a two-lane highway for a mile. McKay was operating entirely at his own risk. The $300,000 invested in the huge ship was all his own money.

No-one dared buy the *Great Republic* on the stocks. Her builder prepared to operate her himself as he had done with the *Sovereign of the Seas*. But this time the fates that had favored him since the launching of the *Flying Cloud* decided that he had tempted fortune once too often. The ship behaved beautifully on her run to New York. There, while she was taking in cargo for her maiden voyage, she caught fire and was burnt to the water's edge. One of mankind's most daring efforts of love and imagination was done for in a few hours. Her insurance policies recovered only about half her value.

Careless writers who accept old tales without checking up on them have copied for years the statement that this was a blow from which McKay never recovered. The best answer to that absurd legend stands plain and obvious in the builder's own record of work well done. Undoubtedly it was a terrible disappointment, but the extent to which it affected his powers can be judged best from the fact that he immediately returned to the job, completing nine large clippers in fifteen months—by far the fastest rate of production of his whole career. Six of these were ordered, or bought on the stocks, by James Baines of Liverpool, who took quick advantage of the recent repeal of the last Navigation Laws to patronize the man whom even Britannia had come to recognize as the greatest master of his art.

As for the quality of the work produced in those fifteen months, look at the record again. One of the new ships, the *Lightning*, sailed 436 miles in a day on her first run to Liverpool, the all-time world's record for any sailing ship. Certainly she was not put together by a broken man. Two others, the *James Baines* and *Donald McKay*, made best days' runs of 423 and 421 miles respectively.

And the *Great Republic* herself, in one final interweaving of the careers of the clipper-ship men, was bought by Captain Nat Palmer for A. A. Low and Brother and rebuilt under his supervision to have a remarkable career in spite of her mishap. Captain Nat razeed her down to measure 3356.59 tons and rigged her much more conservatively than McKay had done. But even in these reduced circumstances she was still able to join the other six immortals with her best day's run of 413 miles. If she ever had had a chance in favorable weather, as McKay originally designed her, there is little doubt that she would have proved herself the fastest of all sailing ships.

In addition to the gold rush trades to California and Australia, the early Eighteen Fifties had provided other excitements. Repeal of the Navigation Acts permitted American clippers to enter the China-to-England tea trade, which for two centuries had been monopolized by the British themselves. Nat Palmer's *Oriental*, the first American clipper seen in the port of London, created a tremendous stir. She arrived in the fastest time ever made from China, carrying a full cargo for which she had received almost twice the freight rates that other ships were able to charge. The yacht *America*, at about the same time, proved herself so much the speediest thing of her kind afloat that she started the long British-American rivalry for the *America's* cup. Steamers were improving, but they could not stand up with the clippers in honest competition. The only steamship line which tried to get along on its own earnings failed disastrously. The others were paid big government subsidies, such as the clippers never got. The editor of *Harper's Magazine*, writing in 1851, predicted "—if our steam men do not look to their oars—a return to the old and wholesome service of wind and sail. . . . It is taking nature in the fullness of her bounty, and not cramping her gifts into boiling water-pots."

But California began to grow her own food. Steamers improved bit by bit. Panic swooped on the exchanges in 1857. With freight rates tumbling, the spar-smashing risks of the great voyages became too costly, and the beautiful wind ships entered upon their long twilight. McKay aided in developing a new type of ship, the medium clipper, distinctly fast but with a far greater comparative carrying capacity.

Looking back on his triumphs, he could write, "I never yet built a vessel that came up to my own ideal; I saw something in each ship which I desired to improve." That is about as much as we can learn of his inmost secret. The portrait made in the year when he wrote that shows a remarkable face with the jaw and mouth of a man of action, the wavy hair and brow of a poet, and between the two contrasting aspects a pair of watchful, unsatisfied eyes. The picture helps to explain the miracle of organization that was at the basis of his task. He was not much of an inventor. Slowly and shrewdly he blended other men's ideas until, in those wonderful bursts of assurance that produced at his own risk the *Sovereign of the Seas* and the *Great Republic,* he expressed the knowledge of an indomitable people, and symbolized the American dream.

In comment upon the remarks of detractors who say that the brief usefulness of the clippers betrays their failure as a type, it can be admitted—of course—that normal times call for workaday products which competent men can handle well enough. But now and then, in great emergencies, even close-fisted business demands heroism in the human imagination. Such a demand brought forth the most daring and beautiful objects in the world of practical affairs: the Yankee clippers, wrought by geniuses who expected geniuses to drive them. Even the purse-proud owners for a little while were exalted. Overnight they stopped naming their vessels *Eliza* and *Hope,* and began to call them *Flying Scud, Golden Light, Quickstep, Hotspur.*

A merchant who could name a ship *Lightfoot* (or for that matter, *John Gilpin*) had more than commerce in his soul.

The clippers were half poetry. There will always be those who try to pare down poetic vision to the limits of their own comfortable comprehensions. But genius is never comfortable: it is the impassioned quest for perfection.

For a little while, men of commerce found it profitable to pay for perfection upon the ocean, and found one man who could consistently produce something so close to perfection that the difference is not worth an argument. Nat Palmer and Griffiths, Webb and Pook, all led up to the great climax, but one man proved capable of doing the heroic thing again and again. In himself and in his productions, Donald McKay symbolizes the era when young America announced her power and greatness to a startled world.

INDEX

INDEX

INDEX